Academy *for* Young Ladies

SARAH AND THOMAS BELL,
MATRON AND KEEPER AT THE

Parramatta Female Factory
1836–1843

SUE BELL

Publishing Services by IngramSpark
www.IngramSpark.com

ISBN   Print   978 0 6457778 0 2
         E-Book   978 0 6457778 1 9

A catalogue record for this book is available from the National Library of Australia

Cover: *Entrance to Port Jackson*. William Alexander Miles. Mitchell Library, State Library of NSW, Call no. PXA 537.

Cover design and text layout by Todd Doyle | hakea.co

Some of the images and illustrations in this book may have been edited or enhanced. They have been sourced from scans and photographs, some are the only surviving copy, and others have sustained damage over time. In all cases we have tried to accurately represent the original image or artwork.

Academy *for* Young Ladies

Contents

Illustrations

Instead of manually typing the (often lengthy) links below, we recommend visiting the companion website: **academyforyoungladies.com**

Preface

This is the story of Thomas and Sarah Bell, my paternal great-great-grandfather and grandmother, and their early life in New South Wales (NSW) after arriving in 1832. In particular, it tells of their time as keeper and matron of the Parramatta Female Factory.

The family story that was handed down about the Bells' early life in NSW was that Thomas arrived in charge of convicts and then took up land in Queensland. Sarah was never mentioned and I am not sure we even knew her name. Some years ago my sister, Diana Bell, was doing some family research and found information which revealed that both Sarah and Thomas had worked at the Parramatta Female Factory after arriving in NSW. This new information led my sister and me to the NSW State Archives where we confirmed that Sarah had been the matron and Thomas the keeper at this factory in the 1830s and early 1840s. To our delight we located letters in the Parramatta Female Factory files which were written by our great-great-grandparents.

I was hooked and decided to write Sarah's story thinking how lucky I was to have a female ancestor who had not disappeared from history. However, I discovered that although Sarah was the matron at the Parramatta Female Factory, Thomas as the male was always really the one in charge. Most newspaper reports and official correspondence referred to him in relation to the factory.

Consequently, this story is of both the Bells, following Professor Noeline Kyle's advice that, in order to find the women, you need to find traces of the men.[1]

The main incentive for writing about Sarah and Thomas Bell is that I believe theirs is an intriguing story which deserves to be recorded and preserved. I also want to provide my family with an account of their ancestors' emigration to NSW and their early life in Australia, and in particular their time as administrators at the Parramatta Female Factory.

Introduction

Thomas and Sarah Bell came to NSW from Ireland. Thomas Bell was born in Killcullen, County Kildare in 1798 to Thomas Bell and Elizabeth Marsh and it appears that the Bell family may have come originally from Yorkshire. Sarah Bell (née Alexander) was born near Gort in County Galway in 1803 and was the second daughter of John Alexander, whose family had come originally from Scotland, and of Mary Mahon. Sarah and Thomas married in Dublin in 1819 and had five children.

Their children were born in different counties which suggests that the Bells may have moved around. Mary Isabella was born in the town of Tullamore, King's County (now County Offaly) on 14 October 1825, Joshua Peter in the town of Kilcullen, County Kildare on 27 January 1827, and John Alexander on 23 January 1828 and Marmaduke on 13 July 1829 in Queen's County (now County Laois). Their last child, Sarah Elizabeth, was born on 27 August 1831 but there is no record of where she was born.[2]

Record of the children's births from the Bell Family Bible.

This story recounts the Bells' departure from Ireland, their early years in Sydney, their appointments to the Parramatta Female Factory and their life after the factory. An invaluable resource in telling their story has been the letters written to and by the Bells during their time at the factory (many of which are in their handwriting), as well as records of convict women and other staff who were at the factory during their administration. When referring to convict women, I have used their name, the ship they arrived on (in italics) and the date of arrival (in brackets).

A number of authors have written extensively on the early years of the Parramatta Female Factory. However, there are few secondary sources that specifically mention the Bells and cover the years when the Bells were administrators of the factory: from August 1836 to February 1838, under Governor Richard Bourke; and from August 1838 to August 1843 under Governor George Gipps. [3]

Their administration coincided with a period of prison reform in Britain and Governor Gipps' attempts to improve the self-sufficiency of the factory. It was also during this period where there was a steady increase in the number of female convicts in the factory, with numbers doubling from 590 women and 134 children when they commenced at the factory in 1836, to 1,203 women and 263 children in July 1842. The British Government's decision to end the transportation of convicts to NSW in 1840 should have reduced numbers at the factory, but this was closely followed by another decision in 1841 which terminated the system of assigning convicts to settlers. This meant that women could no longer leave the factory unless they had a ticket-of-leave, their certificate of freedom or got married.[4]

The final chapter of this document covers Thomas' move to Queensland. Sarah died in 1853 and Thomas relocated to Ipswich in Queensland where he spent the last 20 years of his life. His business interests were run as a partnership under the firm name of Bell and Sons: Thomas and his sons Joshua Peter, John Alexander and Marmaduke. Joshua became the dominant figure, taking over the management of the family company and entering the Queensland Parliament.[5]

Drawings of Parramatta

The sepia pen and wash drawings used to illustrate this story have been held with various members of the Bell family for over 160 years. Why our family had these illustrations was unknown, although the family story was that these drawings were the work of someone titled! After carrying out research at the Mitchell Library in Sydney, I found out that they had been done by William Augustus Miles who was Sydney's Superintendent or Commissioner of Police from 1841 to 1848. The rumour at the time was that he, or his father, was the illegitimate son of William IV of England, so perhaps this was the link to the titled illustrator.

William Miles wrote a journal during this period, *The Registry of Flashmen*, in which he alleged that most of Sydney crime was the result of former convicts mixing with free immigrants. He spent time travelling around the area sketching scenes and creating a visual diary. He was a very competent artist and was on the founding committee of the Society of Artists, formed in March 1850 to encourage colonial art and included, 'nearly all the professional colonial artists, and several amateurs.'

William died in April 1851, substantially in debt, and his wife, Sarah, was left in a dire financial position. Her nephew, Dr William Dorsey, who lived in Ipswich, which at that time was in the north of NSW, helped her with a small allowance for the remainder of her life.[6]

The connection to the Bell family was through Dr Dorsey's daughter, Margaret, who married Thomas and Sarah's second child, Joshua, in February 1861. Sarah Miles died two years later, and the drawings were probably packed up in Sydney, with any of her remaining personal possessions, and shipped to Ipswich where they remained with Dr Dorsey until his death in 1878. They were subsequently passed through generations of the family, deteriorating but surviving, probably through a dose of good luck. It was hoped these drawings would be placed in safe keeping at a library available for future generations. At this stage, it is unknown what has become of them.

William Augustus Miles

Fortunately, I had taken photos of those illustrations that Miles had completed in and around the Parramatta area, and have used them to illustrate this work. He always wrote a description of the subject beside or underneath each illustration and often included an amusing anecdote.

Perhaps Sarah and Thomas Bell met William Miles, although his illustrations of the Parramatta area may have been completed during a trip there after the Bells had left the factory. As they were contemporaries, and there is some correspondence in the factory records relating to William Miles, they probably knew of each other. However, they would never have imagined there would be a family connection through the drawings that Miles so carefully created and which would be held for 160 years by the Bells' descendants.[7]

CHAPTER I.

Little death of emigration

'It is all I could expect from a d——
Paramatta Factory b—————— like you'.

Mr Pearce uttered these words on 17 September 1853 at the small settlement of Drayton near Toowoomba, in the north of the colony of New South Wales (NSW). *The Moreton Bay Courier*, carefully removing any offensive words, reported that Leonard Lester, a magistrate, was with Joshua Bell on the verandah of the Royal Bull's Head Inn and had witnessed Pearce walking across from Mr Mehan's Inn where he had been drinking. Joshua, the eldest son of Sarah and Thomas Bell, was a magistrate from the Dalby Police Office and it appeared that Pearce was not happy with a judgement Joshua had made against him the previous day, for his non-payment of two Chinese employees.

The witness stated that when Pearce reached them, he had said:

> I hope, Bell, you feel more independent to-day than
> you did yesterday when sitting on the Bench. You did
> not behave to me on that occasion like a friend … You
> a magistrate? You dirty, low scoundrel. You are a low
> paltry b——.

Joshua attempted to get the 'old fool' to desist but Pearce continued 'calling him a real black guard' and 'a Parramatta b—' and told him that he was 'reared in the factory' and then made some coarse remarks about Joshua's father.

Later, Joshua wrote to Pearce asking him to publicly apologise for these offensive remarks. Pearce agreed to withdraw any statements against Joshua's family but not his comments about Joshua. Consequently, Joshua took action against Pearce for slander and the matter was heard at a sitting of the Supreme Court of NSW at Moreton Bay on 18 May 1854. The Attorney-General, John Plunkett, and Mr Purefoy appeared for Joshua who subsequently received £200 in compensation. [8]

How did Joshua Bell, who had been born in Ireland, end up in one of the far off regions of the colony of NSW? And what was Mr Pearce alluding to in his remarks?

Joshua Bell's parents, Thomas and Sarah Bell, and their five children, Mary Isabella, Joshua Peter, John Alexander, Marmaduke and Sarah Elizabeth, left Dublin for the colony of NSW on 4 December 1831. Why the Bells came to NSW is unclear. They may have been influenced to leave Ireland because the 1830s in Ireland was a period of economic downturn and rapid population growth, with severe food shortages, unemployment and frequent epidemics of infectious diseases such as cholera.

Alternatively, they may have been enticed to leave through the publicity surrounding migration schemes to NSW and Van Diemen's Land being offered by the Emigration Commission. This commission was established in 1831 by the British Government to provide advice on, 'seasons, destination, ages and sexes of potential emigrants' and raise the general knowledge of the population about the benefits of emigration. These schemes sought single women, because the population in NSW was predominantly men, but also married couples with young families seeking opportunities to emigrate. Otherwise, the Bells may have been encouraged to leave Ireland by people who were seeking a new life in the antipodes, such as Samuel Lapham and his wife and child who also came from County Kildare and travelled on the same ship to Hobart Town.[9]

The Bells must have been excited about the new life they were about to undertake but also concerned about taking their young family on such a long and dangerous journey. They must have felt the heartache of departure, often called the 'little death of emigration', and wondered if they would ever see Ireland again.

They travelled to Hobart Town on the ship *Cleopatra*, a brig of 280 tons with a single deck and an E1 rating (E was second out of 5 classes and 1 indicated it was made of materials of first quality). Charles Sweet was the captain and William de Little the surgeon of the five-year-old vessel. [10]

The Bells came as unassisted migrants which meant that they funded their own passages to the colony. Thomas wrote later that he, 'incurred very great expense in coming with my family to this Country'. They travelled as cabin passengers, as did Thomas Reige and Samuel Lapham, Mrs Lapham and their child. Travelling in steerage on the same ship were Mr and Mrs Gee and their three children, T. O. Mara (or O'Mara or Meara), his wife and six children, R. Chandler, as well as 67 Chelsea pensioners and their families. The pensioners were travelling under an arrangement where they commuted their pensions, for an advance of four years' payment, and were given small grants of land in one of the British colonies. Twenty of the Chelsea pensioners left the *Cleopatra* at the Cape of Good Hope which was a British colony at this time. [11]

Three months earlier, James Backhouse, a Quaker, had travelled from London to Van Diemen's Land on the *Science* with a group of Chelsea pensioners. He claimed that, before leaving port, the pensioners received part of their advance from the government and, 'wasted their money in strong drink…and became very unruly' and that on the voyage, 'few days passed without some of the pensioners being intoxicated and quarrelling.' [12]

There is no record of the route the *Cleopatra* took, although most emigrant ships travelling to NSW at this time headed south via Tenerife or the Cape Verde Islands and then to Rio de Janeiro or Trinidad. They would then often spend some weeks in the doldrums waiting for the westerly winds to take them to Cape Town in South Africa and then on to NSW.

Four months before the Bells left Ireland, Richard Bourke, the new governor of NSW, left Portsmouth with his family. He was from County Limerick in Ireland and his daughter, Anne Bourke, kept a diary during their voyage which provides an insight into the often trying conditions people experienced on sailing ships at this time. In her diary, Anne recounted the trials and tribulations of sea travel, such as the terrifying storms which would have made travellers extremely seasick and afraid:

> Oh such a night as it was, the dreadful lurches on
> one side were terrible, not one of us attempted to go
> to bed, my bed being to windward I knew I should
> be rolled out if I tried to lay down … Sunday night,
> whilst we were at dinner such a tremendous sea came

completely over the hammock nettings, it came such force against one side of the ship and threw her so completely over on the other, that I was not the only person who thought that there would be some difficulty in getting her up again, but being very light and buoyant, after resting on her side for about two minutes she rose gradually in what Capt. Biddle calls a most graceful manner.[13]

The weather would have been very hot as they crossed the Equator and Anne wrote that they often stayed on deck until 10pm seeking cooler air. She described the boredom and monotony of the voyage, particularly when they were 'stuck in the doldrums' and 'lost the trade' (winds) and were becalmed, and then the joy of finally catching the winds and continuing the long trip to Sydney.

It was likely that the Bells had not previously left Ireland, so they would have been amazed by the strange and exotic animals and environments they encountered: tropical islands, sharks, flying fish and strange birds, and also the open sea which must have been both terrifying and exciting:

> This is one of the most beautiful evenings I have ever felt or seen, I could not tear myself from deck … the moon and stars are so bright and everything so quiet, the wind is nice and fair and water very smooth … and all round us we saw every now and then just like fireworks breaking … an immense shoal of porpoises or albacores jumping about in the water and dashing the spray and phosphoric light up so high as to resemble sparks of fire, it had a very beautiful appearance in the gloomy light.[14]

The *Cleopatra* stopped at the Cape of Good Hope to unload some of Chelsea pensioners and take on provisions and left on 17 March 1832. The ship headed across the Indian Ocean towards Van Diemen's Land but, tragically, during this part of the trip, the Bells' little seven-month-old baby Sarah died. We can only imagine the scene as the passengers and crew gathered on the deck while the captain read the burial service and the tiny enshrouded body was slipped overboard into the vast sea. Thomas recorded her death in the Bell Family Bible, writing that, 'her remains are laid in the Indian Ocean between the Cape of Good Hope and Van Diemen's Land.'[15]

On 2 May 1832, not long after their daughter's death, the Bells arrived in Hobart Town after five long months at sea. They continued their voyage to Sydney on the *Harlequin,* arriving on 11 May 1832. Six months before, James Backhouse described sailing into Sydney Harbour:

> A light-house marks the South Head, which is about a mile from the North Head ... The hills, in many places, are covered with Gum-trees and different species of Banksia, and other trees and shrubs, such as are peculiar to this part of the world ... Sydney strikes us as being more like a large English town, than Hobart Town ... the buildings are like those of towns within thirty miles of London. In the court-yards and the gardens of the more retired streets, Peach, Orange and Loquat trees, Grape-vines, and many singular and beautiful shrubs are growing luxuriantly.[16]

The environment of Sydney had changed significantly since the First Fleet landed in 1788, with the construction of many buildings and roads and with free settlers and emancipists now outnumbering convicts. Landing at Sydney Cove in May 1832, the Bells would have seen the original Government House located on the hill in Bridge Street, as the new governor's residence, still standing today, was not completed until 1845.

Government House in 1844. W.A. Miles.

The family was still dealing with the trauma of leaving home, the death of their baby and the gruelling trip to NSW. Their main aim would have been to find accommodation for their family. In the first instance, this may have been in one of the inns or hotels in Sydney which provided short term accommodation. This accommodation may have been near George Street because six months later, 'a blast was fired in George street, opposite the lumber yard and out of the stones propelled into the air, one weighing upwards of twelve pounds, fell at the feet of a son of Mr Bell's aged five years.'[17]

Thomas had been working in the vicinity since July 1832, so the family may have been living nearby. John Alexander Bell, who would have been five years old, may have been the child who had the lucky escape.

As the Bells settled into life in Sydney, they would have been very aware that they had arrived in a penal settlement. Gangs of male convicts would have been going to work in the lumber yard and a few weeks after their arrival, they may have seen female convicts who had just disembarked from the *Burrell*. They also may have ventured into the wilderness surrounding Sydney and seen unfamiliar vegetation and strange animals, such as the emu which the artist William Miles described as, 'that great overgrown turkey'.[18]

'My first sketch at the Antipodes.- that Emu!- that great overgrown turkey!' W.A. Miles.

CHAPTER 2

An administrator in the colony

Thomas wasted no time in finding a job. On 4 July 1832, he commenced as a clerk in the Master Attendants (Harbour Master's) Office, on an annual salary of £91. The office consisted of: harbour master, John Nicholson, a deputy harbour master, a master builder, two clerks, two superintendents and two pilots, with a total annual budget of £1,500. Thomas claimed later that he had, 'brought many recommendatory letters from the Govt', and used one he had obtained from Lord Howick to secure this job. [19]

At the time of Thomas' appointment, the British Government commenced a trial of a government assistance scheme to bring free women to the colony. Emigration had been actively discouraged since the beginning of the colony of NSW. By this time, with a population which was overwhelmingly male, the government decided to address the shortage of women through the introduction of an emigration scheme to bring female migrants to the colony. This was funded by the decision of the British government in 1831 to sell Crown land in the colonies.

Thomas had only been at the Harbour Master's Office a month and a half when he was appointed to an additional role of managing the accommodation for the first female emigrants coming to NSW on the *Red Rover*. The accommodation was in the main building of the lumber yard recently vacated by the convicts from

Hyde Park Barracks. They had been employed there in various trades, such as carpenters and wheelwrights, before being moved to a smaller site next to the barracks. The lumber yard building was in very poor condition, yet it could house significant numbers of women, and with its high fence, it would hinder prying eyes.

Governor Bourke knew the building was sub-standard but rationalised that the *Red Rover* was a trial and that further emigration may not eventuate. He also justified that it was:

> superior in such accommodation to the Ship the women had just left, and to the dwellings of many of them in the Countries of their birth … [although did acknowledge that many of the women] … had probably been accustomed to better lodging - and better fare than was here provided for them. [20]

The *Red Rover* arrived in Sydney on 14 August 1832 with 202 women and girls, many of whom came from charitable institutions in Cork and Dublin. *The Sydney Monitor* wrote, 'so many females weeping at the loss of their country and relations, and under the deep feelings of lonely friendlessness, was touching.' [21]

They were permitted to take their beds and blankets from the ship and walk 'two and two' to the old lumber yard. The lodgings must have been dreadful, as one woman wrote to her father that:

> When we arrived at the lumber-yard, - oh! of all the places in the world, it was the worst. No place to sit down: the whole set to sleep in one place, just like a stable, only not so clean. [22]

These women would have been completely dislocated in this foreign land. A Ladies Reception Committee, made up of the wives or daughters of 'important' people, such as Anne Bourke, was appointed to help complete paper work and advise the women on employment. By 2 October 1832, only 17 women remained in the lumber yard. These women had found it difficult to find jobs, or to find alternative work when their employment proved unsatisfactory. Colonial Treasurer, Campbell Riddell, discovered when visiting the lumber yard that there was only sufficient rations for twelve women and that Thomas had, 'some of them victualled from his own table.'

Riddle suggested that Thomas should be given approval to order provisions for those who returned and that the women should be encouraged to go to Bathurst where there was a shortage of free female servants. Perhaps they took his advice because, by January 1833, there were no women in the accommodation. [23]

Thomas managed these lodgings for over three months during 1832, although his name only appears in the *Returns of the Colony* (Blue Books, 1832) as a clerk in the Harbour Master's Office. He had assistance from James Sparkes per *England (*1826), who had been a watchman at the previous lumber yard and later petitioned Governor Bourke for recompense for this extra work. [24]

After the experiment with free women arriving on the *Red Rover,* the London Emigration Committee (LEC) implemented the scheme, with fourteen ships arriving at Sydney, Hobart and Launceston between 1833 and 1837. The first ship was the *Bussorah Merchant* which arrived in Sydney on 11 August 1833. Despite Thomas' new appointment as Assistant Superintendent of Carters' Barracks in July of that year, which was, 'highly recommended to the Governor', he once again managed the women's accommodation at the lumber yard. [25]

By the time the third ship, the *David Scott,* arrived the women were being housed in temporary lodgings next to the Sydney Bazaar. Governor Bourke complained about the cost of £222 12s 9d to rent this building and the £12 10s paid to Thomas Bell for managing the accommodation. [26]

When the next ship, the *Duchess of Northumberland,* arrived on 27 February 1835, Thomas was once again in attendance. The process of employing the women was chaotic, with Thomas complaining that even though the colonial treasurer and the collector of internal revenue helped with the 'disposal' of women, four women were, 'taken away without my knowledge by some of the ladies of the committee the day of their arrival … in the midst of great confusion'. *The Sydney Gazette* praised those involved:

> Out of the 240 young girls … there are only twenty-six to be provided with situations … [and] only four left their places, (two of whom were ill) and returned to the Bazaar …There is a great deal of credit due to the Colonial Treasurer and Mr. Bell of Carters' Barracks, for their exertions to provide them with respectable employers. [27]

Thomas' role in managing this accommodation ended on 1 January 1836 when he was promoted from Assistant Superintendent to Superintendent of the House of Corrections on a salary of £50 and Keeper of the Debtors' Prison on a salary of £100 (plus accommodation), both located at Carters' Barracks. His appointment was greeted with approval, 'Mr. Bell takes his place, who, from his high character and respectability, will, we have no doubt, give general satisfaction.' In the assistant's role he had been provided with somewhere to live. This must have been a big benefit for the family although it is not clear whether it was in the barracks or elsewhere. However, wherever it was, it surely would have been basic housing, particularly if it was in the barracks, and may have only been one room for the whole family.[28]

Carters' Barracks.

The barracks had been built in 1820 on what is now Central Railway Station, between the Brick Works and the old Burial Ground. It had previously been barracks for 200 male convicts who transported carts full of bricks from the brickworks to building sites, and workshops for 100 convict boys (mostly between 14 and 16 years of age), who trained to work as tradesmen and government apprentices. In 1823, two treadmills were installed at these barracks (one worked by 36 men, the other by 20 men) to undertake the backbreaking work of grinding corn.

By the time of Thomas' appointment, all the boys had been assigned to settlers and the barracks had been converted into accommodation for mounted police, quarters for a chain gang of convict men and a Debtors' Prison. This prison commenced operating in December 1835 after new rules were introduced which permitted debtors, who had the means, to live outside the gaol in George Street. Consequently only the 27 debtors, without means, were moved from the gaol to Carters' Barracks in December, which had been, 'fitted up with every attention to the comfort and health of the debtors.' [29]

Soon after Thomas took up his new position, he defended himself in the Supreme Court against an accusation of assault by William Corp, a debtor. Evidence in the case revealed that each debtor could purchase a pint of wine each day with money earned from their trade and/or received from their creditors, who were encouraged to contribute a weekly sum for their support. Thomas refused to give Corp his daily allowance of wine because he assumed, from Corp's conduct, that he'd had enough wine. Thomas, facing abuse from Corp, sent for a constable, who had him handcuffed. Corp argued this was assault. The jury returned a verdict in favour of Thomas, with Justice Dowling observing that this case had exposed abuses (presumably with alcohol) which should cease immediately. [30]

The Bells would have been keen for their children to be educated and in January 1835 they enrolled their eldest son, Joshua, who had just turned eight, at Sydney College. This college had just opened and Joshua is listed in the register as its second student. Many of the boys were sponsored and, in Joshua's case, he was supported by Thomas Barker, a member of the College Council. John and Marmaduke began a year later with John sponsored by

R Murphy (possibly Roger Murphy) and Marmaduke by William Wentworth. It is not clear if, or where, Mary Isabella went to school as she was about nine years of age when the family moved to Carters' Barracks. [31]

Having her sons, and possibly her daughter, at school would have given Sarah some free time. She may have taken the opportunity to earn an income by teaching piano. On 9 September 1833, a Mrs Bell advertised that she, 'had leisure to instruct a few more pupils on the PIANO FORTE' and that, 'Any commands left at Mr. Ellard's Musical Warehouse, would be attended to.' This could have been Sarah because four years later, on 18 December 1837, when the Bells were about to leave their positions at the Parramatta Female Factory, she advertised for sale, 'A New Pianoforte, only a few months in use. It is on the newest principle, including Metallic Plate, &c. Apply to Mrs. Bell, Female Factory, Parramatta.' [32]

As settlers in the colony, the Bells could apply to have convicts assigned to them as servants and it appears they took advantage of this opportunity to obtain help in the household. In August 1834, *The Sydney Gazette* reported that Ann Davis per *Burrell* (1831), who had been assigned to Thomas, had been missing for about ten days. She was described as, '25, Spain, washerwoman 4 feet 9, fair ruddy comp. brown hair, grey full eyes, nose sharp at the point, nail of left little finger disfigured.' It is not clear if she ever returned. Two months later, Selina/Celina McGarry per *Southworth* (1832), who was probably Ann Davis' replacement at the Bells' residence, was charged with being absent all night without leave. This 'little dumpy Patlander' (a derogatory term for an Irish person) was given one month in third class at the Parramatta Female Factory and she was to be returned to the Bells' service once her sentence expired. Selina announced on hearing her sentence, 'I won't come back your Honor', and was cautioned to be more respectful to the court. She repeated the words and was accused of contempt of court, receiving an additional two months to her original term of transportation. [33]

A year later, Thomas was back in court, this time charging Ann Putter per *George Hibbert* (1834) with insolence and disobeying orders. She stated that she, 'was only allowed brown bread to eat, and a straw bed to sleep on, both of which she considered unbefitting her situation of a useful servant.' She received two months in third class at the factory, with a recommendation to be assigned, in future, 'up the country.' [34]

Did these women have real grievances with unscrupulous behaviour from the Bells? The treatment of assigned convicts by settlers differed, with some treating them in a ruthless and callous way and others with kindness and understanding. Many female convicts were not afraid of their settlers and did in fact have recourse to report to a magistrate any behaviour that they considered mistreatment. If the courts proved them correct, they could receive a period in a female factory and/or reassignment to a settler who may be more accommodating to their needs. Unfortunately for Selina McGarry, she was to be returned to the Bells after her term in the Parramatta Female Factory. Ann Putter, on the other hand, was reassigned 'up the country' with no guarantee that another settler would be kinder or more understanding.

After three and a half years at Carters' Barracks, Thomas and Sarah received the good news that they had been appointed as keeper and matron of the Parramatta Female Factory. Thomas had gained experience with housing female migrants as well as managing the House of Corrections and the Debtors' Prison at the

Carters' Barracks. Sarah, on the other hand, does not appear to have had experience managing convicts. She is not listed in the Blue Books as holding a government position since arriving in NSW although, perhaps, she helped her husband at Carters' Barracks.

This lack of experience, combined with the complexity of the roles they were about to take on, could have been indicators of possible problems at the factory during their administration.

CHAPTER 3.

'Cheering intelligence of the factory':

APPOINTMENT *of the* BELLS *to the* FEMALE FACTORY

About 25,000 female convicts were sent to NSW and Van Diemen's Land during the transportation era and about 9,000 of them spent some time in one of the female factories in the colonies. These female convicts were considered by some to come from a criminal class in Britain. However, for about 64 percent of women transported from 1826 to 1840 this was their first offence, 28 percent had one previous short term crime and 6 percent had two former offences. Fewer than 3 percent had offended more than twice. These women were, 'casual offenders taking advantage of what chance openings they encountered, be they in their mistress's quarters, at home laundering sheets, in a dressmakers' workroom, on the street or in a shop'. [35]

The first Parramatta Female Factory opened in 1804 with two small rooms above the Parramatta Gaol. Women housed in this factory were waiting to be assigned to free settlers, the birth of a child or punishment for misdemeanours they had committed since arriving in the colony. While there, they were expected to undertake some sort of work, such as spinning wool. This factory became overcrowded very quickly and, in 1818, Governor Macquarie ordered the construction of a new building.

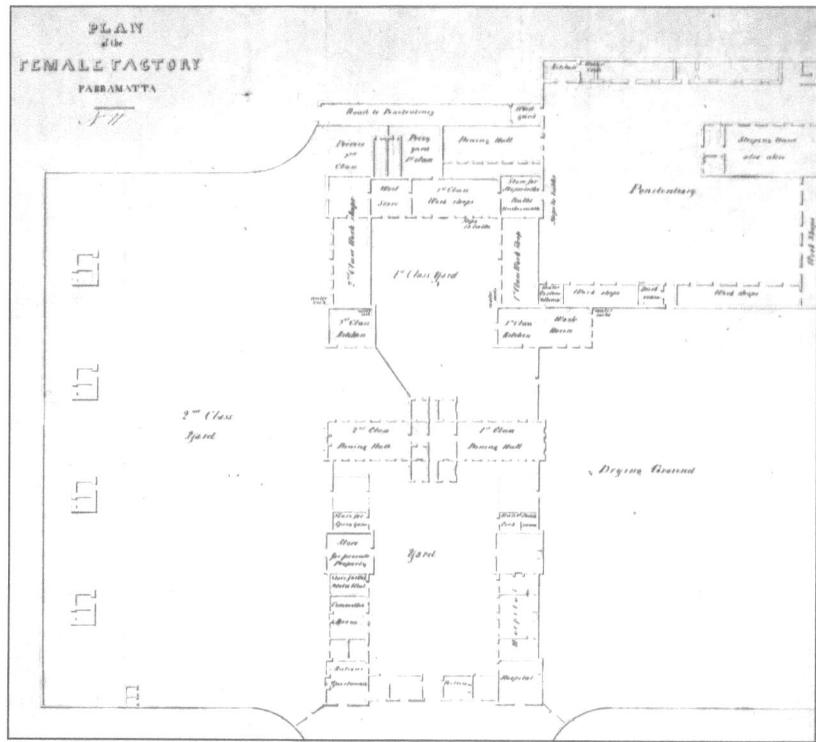

William Buchanan plan of the Female Factory, November 1833

This building opened on 1 February 1821 designed around Governor Macquarie's regulations of dividing the women into two classes, the crime class and other class. It had three storeys with the ground floor used as the first and second class dining halls and the upper two floors used as the sleeping dormitories for 300 female convicts; first class women were housed on the right and second class women on the left with a double stairway in the middle of the building so the girls from either class would not mix. Behind this main building, connected by a fence, were the kitchens for the first and second classes and workshops. In front of the building, on the left, was the matron's quarters and meeting rooms and on the right the hospital which had various wards and a dead room at the back. The factory was on four acres of land surrounded by a nine-foot stone wall (later increased to 15 feet) and moat. In 1823 Governor Brisbane, who had taken over from Governor Macquarie, added a two-story building in a separate yard to the north-west as a prison wing for 60 female convicts. [36]

On becoming governor in 1825, Sir Ralph Darling decided to classify women into three classes, in order to distribute resources based on good behaviour and to reflect the many roles of the factory. First class women were given a better food allowance, higher quality clothing, were able to receive visitors, attend church and could marry. Second class women could not be assigned because they had children, were old and/or ill, pregnant or had committed some minor criminal offence while on assignment. They had inferior food, unless pregnant, and fewer privileges. Third class women had either reoffended or were free women sentenced in NSW. They lived in the prison wing, performed hard labour such as breaking stones for roads, received inferior rations and clothing and, from 1826, had their hair shaved. [37]

Ann Gordon was matron of the factory when Major General Sir Richard Bourke arrived as the new governor of NSW in December 1831. The factory appeared to be operating smoothly until 1836 when colonial newspapers began publishing lurid stories about the immoral conduct of members of Ann Gordon's family and attacking policies which they believed encouraged misbehaviour among the women. Governor Bourke decided to dismiss Mrs Gordon without any blame but because he wanted to:

> place the Factory at Parramatta upon an entirely new footing. The numbers ... have rendered the place much more a Gaol than an Asylum, and it requires in

> consequence the Government of a Prison. A matron
> alone is not sufficient to the task of controlling
> and superintending so large a number of Prisoners.
> I propose therefore to place a Man and his Wife at
> the Head of the Establishment, the one as Keeper the
> other as Matron with a sufficient number of Male and
> Female Turnkeys … [38]

The governor appointed Thomas as keeper (administering stores and buildings) and Sarah as matron of the factory in August 1836 whose, 'behaviour in other situations of trust I had reason to be fully satisfied'. This comment would no doubt have related to Thomas who had experience with managing convicts and female migrants. [39]

Thomas was appointed on a salary of £200 per annum 'with apartments' and Sarah, as matron, received £100 which significantly increased the family's income. However, previous matrons had each received £150 per annum so Governor Bourke, by reducing Sarah's salary, showed clearly that Thomas was in charge and not just of stores and buildings. This was a risky strategy as Elizabeth Fry, one of the main promoters of prison reform in Britain, had been lobbying the British Government about the importance of having a woman, familiar with the treatment of female prisoners, as head of every female prison.

The position of matron at the factory was unusual in that it had an official identity and salary. Women at that time who were employed by government normally performed work in lowly positions such as an office keeper, nurse or female turnkey, all of which were an extension of domestic service. For a woman to hold any senior management role was virtually unknown at this time, so matrons of female factories would have been Australia's highest paid nineteenth century female public servants. Nevertheless, Sarah had few rights as, 'Government employment of married women was problematic as the common law doctrine of coverture meant that wives had not legal or economic identity.' In other words, she was considered to be under her husband's protection and authority. [40]

Governor Bourke also adjusted the rest of the workforce at the factory which now consisted of a clerk, three male and four female turnkeys, a porter, a midwife and a school master (or mistress). There were also Anglican and Catholic chaplains (the latter for the first time) who visited the women. The governor's other change was to replace the factory's management committee with a visiting magistrate to the factory because, 'the discipline of the place, which never was good, became relaxed, and a reform in the Institution was evidently required.' [41]

Pieter Laurentz Campbell, Police Magistrate at Parramatta, was appointed as visiting magistrate of the factory. This became an additional responsibility for him and he was expected to be an, 'auditor, inspector, arbitrator, magistrate, bursar and to present a monthly report on conditions at the Factory.' He inspected the factory twice weekly, checked all records, punished prisoners if their misdemeanours were outside the matron's authority and resolved any disturbance at the factory. Julia Leach, the matron in 1838, wrote scornfully that, 'The Visiting Magistrate over me comes twice in the week stopping just a few minutes, & has very little better idea of the difficulty of managing them or the support I require than a person in England.' John Clapham, storekeeper at the same time, agreed complaining that, 'a young inexperienced man who is a Magistrate & receives £100 a year for riding from his own house twice a week to sign his name in a book at the Factory.' [42]

Parramatta River. W.A. Miles.

Sarah and Thomas would have been pleased with their new positions as they both now received salaries as well as accommodation for their family. Thomas was invited to inspect the factory soon after their appointments, and, although Sarah is not named, she probably accompanied him. The management committee was informed that they were to provide him with 'relevant instructions' during his visit. [43]

The Bells may have come by steamer and walked the couple of miles from the landing place on the Parramatta River to the factory. John Backhouse had travelled by river to Parramatta in the same year and described the environment:

> the shores are low and muddy, and the contiguous
> lands cleared and cultivated. Houses are interspersed

at moderate distances; some of them are inhabited by prosperous settlers, and have the aspect of those of English gentlemen. [44]

Parramatta. Landing Place. W.A. Miles.

Ann Gordon had been asked to vacate the matron's apartments by 31 August 1836. These apartments, which included the matron's office and dispensary, were on the ground floor; the second floor of this building was added in the 1870s, as were the bay windows. It must have been cramped with the Bells' four children as Mary Isabella was almost 11, Joshua was 9, John Alexander was 8 and Marmaduke was 7. Joshua, John and Marmaduke had left Sydney College and Joshua was enrolled at King's School, Parramatta. John was not enrolled at Kings until 1839 and there is no record of Marmaduke ever attending Kings. [45]

Matron's quarters, 2011

The Bells commenced their jobs on 1 September 1836. Governor Bourke gave instructions that the current storekeeper, William Tuckwell, was to be retained at the factory for a month, 'as a matter of present convenience'. This was probably to provide some continuity in the administration of the factory. Even with this assistance, the Bells, particularly Sarah who presumably had less experience, must have found managing the 590 women and 134 children, who were in the factory at the time, a formidable task.[46]

A month after their arrival, a number of women in the factory attempted to escape at night so they could attend the races the next day. They were not successful. They must have still been disturbed the next day as soldiers from the guard at Parramatta had to be brought in to keep order. This would have been a rude awakening for the Bells and would have highlighted the difficult tasks they were undertaking. [47]

The perennial problem with the factory was that it was expected to serve many roles as:

> not only a gaol, but a house of asylum and probation, a home for the incapacitated (infirm, aged, blind, nursing mothers), a labour exchange, a marriage bureau, a hospital and a manufactory. As each of these functions requires a different physical and administrative organisation to fulfil its purpose, the effective and efficient running of the Factory was virtually impossible, and created as many problems as it solved.' [48]

The term, female factory, presumed that the women were producing something within its walls. In its early days, it had been seen primarily as a manufactory (factory), rather than a penitentiary, where women would be occupied and also earn an income for the government. Governor Bourke's intention was for first class women to undertake needlework, second class women to staff the laundry and hospital, and third class to crush rocks for the streets of Parramatta.

When James Backhouse visited the factory, a month after the Bells took over, he reported that the women:

> are nearly destitute of employment. Formerly, women of this character were employed in spinning, and in weaving coarse, woollen cloth, but this occupation has been abandoned. The rooms where it was carried on, are empty, …The assignable women were occupied with needlework, and the place they were in was clean. [49]

Many convict women were assigned immediately at the ship docks on their arrival in NSW and never went to the factory. Those not assigned, were transferred to the factory where the matron prepared lists of those eligible for assignment which were sent to the governor for his endorsement. Settlers could apply to have a convict woman assigned to them and the matron would select a woman from the list. In fact, Thomas appears to have handled much of the paperwork relating to assignment and other administrative issues during this period of the Bells' administration. [50]

The assignment system was critical to the government as, once women were assigned, they became the responsibility of the settler and were removed from government stores. There were many critics of the assignment system and they often blamed the women:

> *This* is the system which requires alteration: not the interior of the Factory — not its rules and regulations — not the food or raiment— the employment, or the degree of labor ... so long as *assignment* is the order of the day with intractable, demoralized, and ignorant persons of this class, so long will every Penitentiary, no matter of what character, be crowded. [51]

Assignment for the women was a lottery. Many women had genuine issues with their employers and were treated very badly. Even those settlers who treated the women well, would often return them for a range of petty offences, such as absences without leave or insolence which should have been easily resolved.

The assignment system functioned through a number of rules and regulations. One of these regulations was that if a female convict was sent to the factory for an offence while assigned to a settler, the latter, had to reapply for her with a form signed by a magistrate, within seven days from the end of her sentence. Ellen Pollard per *Burrell* (1832) was assigned to Henrietta Howell, a washerwoman in Castlereagh Street, Sydney and was charged with being absent without leave. At Ellen Pollard's trial in March 1837, Mrs Howell stated that her son had reprimanded Ellen for 'remissness' and she (Ellen) called him some 'ill names'. Ellen was sent to the factory and, at the end of her sentence, was assigned elsewhere. Thomas explained that Mrs Howell had not reapplied for her, as per regulation and in the past he had returned women without having received an application from a settler and, 'found many of them [settlers] change their minds, and refuse them, which left me liable to be charged for their fare in the Steamer.' Ellen Pollard was subsequently returned to Mrs Howell. [52]

In some cases convict women were assigned to their husbands who were free. Sometimes all did not go well and their wives ended up in the factory. Their husbands had to reapply for them once they had completed their sentences. In October 1837, Patrick McCallaghan, a gardener for Captain Frederic Ebhart in the Botany Bay area, wrote a memorial to the governor asking for his wife Eliza McGallaghan (or Smith) per *Lady Rowena* (1826) to be released from the factory. He explained that she had been sent there for twelve months for improper conduct in June 1837 and asked that, because her behaviour had been exemplary in the factory, she be assigned to the Ebharts and 'entirely removed' from the bad influences of her shipmates in Sydney. Captain Ebhart supported his memorial. Thomas confirmed her good behaviour in the factory. He did note that she had previously received mitigation for a sentence in the factory and, on reassignment, had reoffended and received her current sentence. Governor Bourke supported

36/9603 - 11th November 1836
           Female Factory Parramatta
               10 th Nov 1836

Sir

In reply to your letter of the 8th instant No 36/258 I have the honor to state that the application of Luke Taylor of Castlereagh Street Sydney for the woman named in the margin [Bridget Sheedey] was recommended by the third Police Magistrate,

(H. F. Gisborne Esq.) -

         I am Sir
      Your most obedient servant
         Thomas Bell
           Keeper

The Honorable
The Colonial Secretary

Thomas Bell to Colonial Secretary re Bridget Sheedey
10 November 1836

the memorial adding ominously that, if she reoffended, 'she will meet with no mercy.' [53]

Another husband, Philip Dwyer per *Chapman* (1836), was not so keen for his wife, Mary Ann McKenna per *Roslin Castle* (1830), to be reassigned to him. However, he did want the money he believed she had stolen from him. He was an innkeeper at Sign of the Rock at Coshill in Liverpool and wrote to the colonial secretary saying that he suspected his wife of robbing him and that the money had been given to Thomas when she was admitted to the factory. Mr Moore, JP, endorsed his request and asked Thomas to return the £1 35s. Thomas replied that, 'Any money brought to the Female Factory by any Prisoner is forfeited by order of His Excellency the Governor [and] it is contrary to my instructions to return it.' It is not clear from the remaining documents what happened to the money. [54]

Some settlers failed to fulfil their responsibilities under the assignment system and were not permitted to have any more servants. Soon after arriving at the factory, Thomas provided documentation on the assignment of Bridget Sheedey per *Hooghley* (1831) and Bridget Hanly per *Surry* (1833). Bridget Sheedey had been sent to Luke Taylor, a shoe binder of Castlereagh Street, Sydney but in November 1836, Bridget was brought before the bench and charged with 'highly improper conduct'. She had accompanied, with her mistress' permission, a man named Cooper for 'improper purposes' and this man was robbed (probably by Bridget) when they returned to her master's house. The police magistrate recommended that Luke Taylor should not be permitted to have more servants as they were, 'very improper persons to have such indulgence.' Bridget Hanly was also before the bench in the same month, charged with drunkenness and her mistress, Dorothy Foster, admitted that, 'she herself had been drinking rum with the prisoner' so Foster was also judged an inappropriate person to have a servant. Both Bridgets were returned to the factory. [55]

The Bells would also have needed to keep up with any amended, or new, regulations overseeing assignment. A regulation was introduced soon after the Bells arrived at the factory which prevented female convicts being assigned to people who kept public houses. Eliza Thompson per *Competitor* (1828) had been assigned to Solomon Levein who leased Pulteney Hotel in Sydney. Eliza was returned to the factory for a misdemeanour and, on her release, Thomas notified Levein that she could not be assigned to him again because of the new regulation. Levein argued that Eliza had been assigned to him before this regulation was introduced and he wanted her returned. Governor Bourke agreed but Eliza had already been assigned to Thomas Watson at H.M. Customs. The governor conceded that any change now would create an awkward precedent. [56]

Many women arrived at the factory with children, while others were pregnant on arrival and gave birth at the factory hospital. This was Australia's first dedicated women's hospital where sick and injured female convicts of all ages (including poor and destitute women) were cared for and where pregnant women could have their babies. It would have been a dangerous and frightening place for women, particularly those who were pregnant, as it would have been unsanitary, usually overcrowded and operated before anaesthesia and antibiotics had been discovered. There were typically about 30 to 40 women in the hospital at this time and with the matron's quarters close by, the Bells would have been very aware of the distress and hardship the women endured there. [57]

Mary Ann Neale was the midwife at the hospital when the Bells arrived. She came to NSW in September 1835 as a free migrant on the *Canton* and, a month after arriving, was appointed as a midwife in the hospital with, 'the most respectable testimonials as to her education and her fitness to perform the duties.' After three months at the factory, Thomas complained that she had, 'repeatedly acted in opposition to the regulations, since I have taken charge.' His complaints were that she had not provided a weekly list of births, had left the factory without seeking permission and was having an 'improper acquaintance' with a man named Tuckwell (previous storekeeper). Mary Ann refuted these accusations although she did leave in March 1837 and Mary Mumford per *Harmony* (1827), who had worked previously at the hospital as a midwife, took over the role. [58]

Those women who arrived at the factory with children, were only meant to keep them until three or four years of age, at which time they were to be sent to one of the orphan schools. However, during the Bells' administration, the orphan schools were becoming overcrowded so this age rule was increasingly relaxed. This meant that there were often a significant number of children at the factory.

In July 1837, Thomas requested permission to send a number of children, aged between five and nine, to the boys' orphan school at Liverpool. They had arrived with their parents on the *Margaret* on 30 May 1837. Official letters focus on the boys' ages, their parents' names, why there had been a delay in forwarding them to the school and whether Thomas had provided correct documentation to Richard Sadleir, Master of the Male Orphan School at Liverpool. The boys were eventually sent by cart as Thomas was, 'very anxious to get Boys of their ages receiving an education'. Nowhere is the tragic parting of these small boys from their mothers acknowledged in the paperwork. [59]

Sometimes, there is a glimpse of sympathy in the myriad of papers committing women and children to their fates. Ellen Ryan per *Asia* (7), was in the factory and because of her age and disability, considered incapable of making a living. Thomas argued that she should go to the Benevolent Asylum where she could be cared for rather than stay in the factory where, 'she is exposed to unnecessary hardship'. Equally, a female migrant, Anne Walsh, arrived unannounced at the factory a month after the Bells commenced, 'with an idea I [Thomas] could take her in, on her presenting herself.' She had arrived on *James Pattison* on 7 February 1836 and had found work with Mrs Robinson of George Street, Sydney who had probably asked her to leave once she found out she was pregnant. Thomas admitted her to the factory, realising she did not have time before the birth of her baby to obtain the necessary order. [60]

A month after the Bells arrived, there were still 590 female convicts and 134 children in the factory. This number was probably larger as it does not capture the turnover of women, with women coming and going constantly. This was particularly evident when a female convict ship arrived and women not assigned to settlers from the ship, were sent to the factory, which led to further overcrowding.

The Bells had two months at the factory before the *Elizabeth*, docked at Port Jackson with 161 women and 27 children. The *New South Wales Government Gazette* advertised for settlers, who wanted female servants, to apply to the superintendent of convicts. Women not assigned directly from *Elizabeth* were sent by steamer to Parramatta. Previously, the steamer had stopped regularly at Squires Brewery at Kissing Point for a liquid refreshment, which was about half way between Sydney and Parramatta. By this date the brewery was closed.

Squires Distilley at Kissing Point -
W.A. Miles

'The first brewery was here

established by a man named

Squires - and the following

couplet in an adjoining church

yard, records that his Beer was

none of the Best. "If you wish

to rot here, Drink Squires Beer."'

The women from the *Elizabeth* arrived at the factory on 26 October 1836. The next day, Thomas wrote that he still did not have assignment lists placing them with settlers so, 'the number of applicants who attended this morning for their servants have in consequence been disappointed.' [61]

One of the convicts on the *Elizabeth*, Mary Gibson, was assigned to Mr Kenwell of Maitland. She had to wait for a steamer to transport her to Maitland so she was sent to Alexander Bushby's house. She escaped and was picked up in George Street, charged with being drunk and having a bottle of rum in her basket, which she claimed had been given to her by a strange man. She was charged with being drunk and sent to third class of the factory for two months. [62]

Two months later the *Pyramus* arrived carrying 120 women and 31 children and, once again, the factory was under pressure to accommodate more women. The problem of overcrowding may explain Pieter Campbell, the visiting magistrate's comment in his third report to the governor on the state of the factory. He complained that there had not been the slightest improvement in the factory's efficiency as a 'Place of Punishment'. [63]

Governor Bourke would have been aware that pressure for prison reform was increasing in Britain and that his changes to make the factory more like a prison may not be popular. He had argued in a despatch to Lord Glenelg, Secretary of State for War and the Colonies, in September 1836 that it would cost more to run the factory with his changes but otherwise it would be a place of, 'mischief and discredit of an ill-conducted Prison.'

By the time Bourke's despatch outlining his changes at the factory reached Lord Glenelg, the latter had already written to the governor. He had received the 1835 Blue Book which contained the statistical returns of the colony for that year, and it revealed that there were 646 women in the factory. Glenelg was astounded there were so many women in the factory, and explained that the last report on the factory had been six years ago, when Governor Darling reported that there had been 537 female convicts which was considered 'inconveniently large'. He expressed his concerns about this and, having heard some of the rumours about Ann Gordon's family, he also questioned the skills of the current officers of the factory to carry out, 'responsible and important duties entrusted to them.' [64]

Lord Glenelg finally received Governor Bourke's September 1836 despatch in May 1837. He approved Bourke's 'alterations' to the factory and increased expenses and although he was sure that the governor had made a:

> careful selection so far as the means existed in the Colony of procuring the services of a suitable Matron … [Glenelg wanted a person] … qualified by recent experience in this country for this responsible charge … [and] … well acquainted with the recent improvements which have been effected in the treatment and discipline of Female Prisoners in this country.

In other words, he intended to appoint new administrators and urged Governor Bourke to find other employment for the Bells. The governor must have been surprised, and probably annoyed, with this news. [65]

Lord Glenelg moved quickly and by July 1837, he notified the governor that he had appointed Julia Leach, as matron, and

John Clapham, as keeper. [66]

Edward Deas Thomson, Colonial Secretary, broke the news to Thomas in November 1837. He firstly praised him and Sarah for the state of the factory, on behalf of the governor, who had visited the factory the day before with Justice Burton:

> The appearance of the women was direct and proper. The Wards Rooms Bedding and Furniture of every kind remarkable clean, the Books of the Establishment in the Clerk's Office extremely well kept and, except for that part of the building still needing repair the whole Establishment appears in excellent order and exhibited very advantageously the care and intelligence with which the Keeper and Matron discharged their respective duties.

He then revealed that their services would no longer be required and that, although the governor was not aware of any current employment, he was sure if something came up that they would meet with, 'favourable consideration of the government.' [67]

Governor Bourke had selected Thomas and Sarah and was reluctant for them to leave. However he had resigned and was about to leave NSW:

> I regret that I have it not in my power to provide any suitable employment for either of these persons, of whose conduct at the Factory, as in former situation under Government, I have the greatest reason to speak in terms of the highest approbation. I venture, therefore respectfully to express a hope that your Lordship will cause the names of Mr. and Mrs. Bell to be brought under the favourable notice

of the officer succeeding to the administration of this Government. [68]

No doubt the Bells were bitterly disappointed. They had only been at the factory for just over a year, and the positions of keeper and matron were senior positions in the public service. By 7 December 1837, two days after Governor Bourke's departure from NSW, Thomas prepared a memorial in which he sought compensation for their dismissal:

> I had served the Government six years - ... the person who succeeded me at Carters Barracks on my removal to Parramatta obtained the permanent situation of Gaoler at Sydney... I had been removed from the Factory without any cause of complaints or without even knowing until within a few days of my Successors arrival that I had been suspended. [69]

Before their departure, *The Sydney Gazette* wrote a flowery assessment of Thomas' administration with no mention of Sarah:

> The appointment of Mr. Bell, however, met with our most cordial approbation. In the various situations he had held under Government we noted with pleasure the assiduity, the suavity, and at the same time the unflinching firmness he invariably displayed; and we anticipated from what we had heard of his character in private life, that he would take speedy means to prevent the Factory, while under his superintendence, from being used as a regular brothel, as it had been under the management of his immediate predecessor. Nor did Mr. Bell's conduct in the management of the Factory falsify our expectations. It is true that from the very inefficient means for the punishment of

the refractory placed at his disposal, as well as from the innate depravity of the vicious subjects placed under his control, Mr. Bell did not make that rapid progress in the reformation of the Factory he would have done under more advantageous circumstances; but, we believe, it will be generally allowed that at no period since the erection of the Factory have its profligate inhabitants been under as good discipline as at present. [70]

Julia Leach and John Clapham, the new appointees, took over as matron and keeper of the Parramatta Female Factory in February 1838, at the same time as Governor Sir George Gipps assumed the position of governor. Governor Bourke's experiment of having a male in charge of the factory had been overturned.

Thomas managed to obtain another position as superintendent of emigrants in the Government Domain which he held from 10 February until 24 August 1838. This accommodation was new and, on his appointment, 116 emigrants were housed there although it could hold about 450 people. A month after Thomas took up the position, there were only 35 people in residence and *The Sydney Monitor* complained of inequity in the handling of government chartered emigrants and privately chartered emigrants. The newspaper argued that privately supported emigrants should be entitled to a week's board and lodging as government emigrants were:

lodged and fed in the new Government quarters in the Government Domain on their landing ... [and should not] ... remain in Government quarters a single day after it has been reported to Mr. Bell that adequate wages and rations (of which he must be left to judge) have been offered ... [71]

It is not clear if the superintendent's position included accommodation for the Bell family. John and Marmaduke Bell returned to school at Sydney College while Joshua stayed at Kings School, probably as a boarder. Perhaps the Bells were not satisfied with the education their sons were receiving, and/or were thinking of moving to the interior of NSW, because four months after taking up this appointment, Thomas placed an advertisement:

> **TUITION A GENTLEMAN** fully competent to teach the Classics, as can be seen from his testimonials and reference, would be happy to devote his unoccupied time to the instruction of Young Gentlemen in the town; or would have no objection to go into the interior as resident Tutor. Application to be made to Mr. Bell, Superintendent of Emigrants. [72]

It is not clear whether anyone answered the advertisement or if the Bells made any concrete plans to move. Regardless, two months later their plans would change.

CHAPTER 4.

'We are in a bad state':

JULIA LEACH *and* **JOHN CLAPHAM**

Julia Leach, the new matron of the factory, came with 'high testimonials' and with experience in the management of female prisoners in England. She was a Christian, possibly a Quaker, as was Elizabeth Fry who supported her selection. John Clapham was appointed house steward and storekeeper at the factory, after being gate-keeper at Coldbath Fields Prison in London. His wife, Agnes, became the schoolmistress. [73]

Julia Leach was paid £130 a year and John Clapham received £150. This created confusion over the respective authority of their positions, even though Lord Glenelg, Secretary of State for War and the Colonies, had made it clear before they left England that, 'the responsibility of the charge of the prisoners should rest with the Matron and that Mr. Clapham should have the general super-intendence of the buildings and the charge of the stores'. [74]

Mrs Leach, and the Clapham family (John, Agnes and their child) arrived on the *Bencoolen* on 23 January 1838, a month before Major Sir George Gipps took over as governor of NSW. On the way to Australia, Mrs Leach and Mr Clapham disagreed strongly about who had the ultimate authority at the factory. This disagreement developed into mutual animosity after they arrived in NSW. [75]

Julia Leach travelled to Parramatta, very soon after landing in Sydney. She arrived, 'unattended upon a wet Saturday to take charge of this strange place - had two good miles to walk after landing from the Steamer'. She was met by, 'Mr Bell who stands more than 6 feet high.'

Elizabeth Fry later explained to Lord Glenelg, that Mrs Leach had gone to the factory before Governor Gipps arrived, 'which accounts for her going there alone & not being properly introduced.' Mrs Leach was aghast at what she saw on her arrival:

> we are in a bad state. There [are] five turnkeys 4 of whom are bigoted Roman Catholics - these five persons are constantly among them - the Roman Catholic Priest is admitted at all hours - to whom they turn my motives inside out ... I have this night within these walls 675 women & upwards of 150 children - they make their escape over the wall with great Ease & away they go - others who do not attempt to get away have means of getting rum - tobacco tea & sugar, & carry on such a traffic as is almost incredible ... The building is just as ill adapted as it can be to effect any good discipline ... I cannot do my duty ... unless I am powerfully supported ... It is unaccountable that the Government does not seriously set to work to prevent such goings on, we have 97 women with children in their arms not one of which scarcely are married. Many of them have two & we have a great many in the family way- it is a complete misery or hot house of crime deeds perpetrated among themselves that I cannot put upon paper, & unless something is done I do not wish to remain. [76]

She wrote to Edward Deas Thomson, Acting Governor, highlighting her concern that:

> idleness [of the third class women was] so extreme it is with the greatest difficulty they have been prevailed upon to cut up sufficient wood to keep the coppers going …. my fear is their indolence will get to so great a height some meal will not be prepared and I am apprehensive of what a scene would then take place and am anxious to prevent. [77]

Governor Gipps visited the factory, soon after taking over as governor in February 1838, and was pleasantly surprised that the women and buildings appeared clean and the women showed him respect. He agreed that there was little employment, except when it was the women's turn to cook, do washing or draw water for the factory.

Pieter Campbell, Visiting Magistrate, agreed there was little employment for the women. He blamed Thomas who, he claimed, had left an outstanding order for hammer handles. Without them, women in third class were unable to split stones which was their only activity. The governor replied that hammer handles were destroyed faster than they could be supplied, which was supported by J F Staff, a staff member at the factory, who said, 'Here they will not work. I know the Governor Sir G. Gipps ordered 70 hammers for them to break stones & the women broke up & destroyed every one of them, immediately & swore they would not work'. [78]

A much greater problem, was the relationship between Julia Leach and John Clapham which had not improved since they arrived in NSW. By mid-March, their quarrel had become so severe, that the employment of both of them at the factory had become untenable. Governor Gipps wrote to Lord Glenelg, highlighting the continuous problem of who had authority at the factory:

> Mr. Clapham accuses Mrs. Leach of various improprieties of conduct and Mrs. Leach retorts upon Mr. Clapham the charge of having attempted to assume over her an authority which, I must say, I think it was never your Lordship's intention to confer upon him. [79]

By April 1838, *The Sydney Herald* raised concerns about Mrs Leach's administration:

> We are afraid that there is something exceedingly rotten in the state of the management of this place … The present matron, Mrs Leach, is doubtless a very respectable woman, but we question if any single female is calculated to manage such an establishment, indeed it requires a man of more than common nerve to be able to control such a number of depraved characters as are congregated within the walls of the Factory. [80]

Eventually, the governor ordered John Clapham to leave and he was replaced by Joseph Snape, who Mr Clapham claimed, 'got beastly drunk was obliged to be carried home & continued to repeat this for several days [and] he was only <u>suspended</u>… he is a Roman Catholic which makes a great deal of difference here.' [81]

Perhaps, in response to his sacking, Mr Clapham accused his predecessor, Thomas, of taking four chairs, a number of sheets and two buckets belonging to government, when he left the factory.

He also claimed Thomas had cut up baby linen to make shirts for his boys and employed two turnkeys to make casks into cases for his use. Thomas disputed these claims, although did admit that he had several chairs with broad arrow markings, instead of his unmarked chairs which were found later in the factory. He also admitted that when his belongings were packed by staff, they had used some old casks and packing cases. In his defence, he said that he had not been present when his luggage was put on drays to be taken to the steamer. This was because he needed to, 'keep tranquility as the prisoners were inclined to be very mutinous on the occasion of my leaving.' [82]

Mr Clapham based his charges against Thomas on evidence provided by the midwife, Mary Mumford, and a female prisoner called 'Sarge'. Thomas discredited Mrs Mumford as a witness. He asserted that before working at the factory, she had been living in a state of adultery with a married man in Parramatta which Thomas claimed he ended when she came to the factory. He maintained that he had to confine her within the walls of the factory, 'on account of her drunken Propensities', her habit of carrying messages and letters from prisoners to their friends outside, and arranging for work to be done by women and then selling it. Thomas also discredited Sarge, by claiming that he had assigned her to a Mrs Mackay of Sydney and, when she proved unsatisfactory, she was returned to the factory. Thomas claimed Mrs Mackay had followed her in order:

> to have her Box or Bundle searched for several articles
> which had been missed from her mistress...[and]...
> on her clothes being searched in the Factory Store,

in presence of myself and Mrs. Mackay a number of
articles of mine as well as Mrs Mackay's were found
sewed up in her gown.

Sarge had been charged and sentenced to 12 months in third
class for each offence. [83]

The Visiting Magistrate, Pieter Campbell, verified Thomas'
defence, reporting that the chairs had been found and that he
believed that the Bells were incapable of appropriating sheets
and linen. He added that he did not trust the witnesses as they
had both been punished by Thomas. He also acknowledged that
when Thomas left, he did not have time to look after his own
baggage, and that it was likely that 'trifling articles' may have been
loaded onto his dray by others, either by accident or for ulterior
motives. He added that Thomas' use of packing cases should not
be begrudged when, 'he was ejected from an office he had every
reason to consider permanent - and how great his losses must have
been in consequence.'

Mrs Mumford admitted that, 'she was always being so pumped
by Mr Clapham that she did say that she had heard such things'.
Sarge said that Mr Clapham had always been very kind to her and,
as he wanted to know the real state of the factory, she thought
it right to tell him. The visiting magistrate suggested that, if the
Bells returned to the factory, Mary Mumford should not remain
as midwife. [84]

At the same time as this was unfolding, Thomas' memorial of
7 December 1837, in which he sought compensation for his
removal, was winding its way through the bureaucracy. [85]

This memorial eventually became immaterial because by July 1838, Governor Gipps acknowledged that, although Mrs Leach was still in charge of the factory, she was, 'so deficient in self-command that I have no hope of being able to retain her.' He terminated her employment to take effect from 24 August 1838, providing her with five months extra pay. [86]

The Colonist announced that Thomas, with no mention of Sarah, had been reappointed to the Parramatta Female Factory, 'from which he had been unceremoniously ousted by the Secretary of State some six or seven months ago, when he had just succeeded in getting the establishment into something like systematic order.' [87]

Governor Gipps must have hoped that the problems at the factory during his first six months in the colony would end, now that the Bells had been reinstated to their positions.

CHAPTER 5

'Change from slothful idleness to cheerful industry':

THE RETURN *of the* **BELLS**

The Parramatta Female Factory had been a focus for Governor Gipps since his arrival in NSW and he must have felt that he had made little progress. *The Sydney Gazette* criticised the appointment of Mrs Leach:

> In no case could the evil of leaving the power of appointing persons to offices of trust and power in the Colonies, in the hands of a Secretary of State some sixteen thousand miles distant, be more strongly exemplified than in the case of the Female Factory. It would be difficult ... to find a person better qualified than Mr. Bell to fill the office of Keeper of the Factory, whether from personal qualifications, or from actual experience. [88]

The Bells resumed their positions at the factory on 24 August 1838, with Thomas as house steward, or storekeeper, and Sarah as matron. This time Sarah was appointed on the same salary as her husband, £150 a year. In doing this, Governor Gipps was implementing Elizabeth Fry's policy, that a woman should run the factory or, realistically, be seen to be running the factory. Her name was also included with the statistics on the State of the Female Factory which appeared regularly in the *NSW Government Gazette,* and she signed most factory correspondence. However, Thomas, as the man, was really seen as the ultimate head of the factory and, to confirm this, in May 1839 Governor Gipps made a decision that, 'subordinate appointments to the factory be given to the House Steward [Thomas] with the approval of the Visiting Justice.' [89]

The Bells moved back into the matron's quarters and enrolled Joshua and John at King's School, Parramatta at the beginning of 1839. It is not clear where their other son, Marmaduke, went to school. The King's School was on the Parramatta River, about one and a half miles from the factory, and included, 'children of Government servants, merchants, tradesmen, innkeepers - in fact all who are desirous of extending to their children the benefit of sound learning and religious education.'

By April 1841, there were 80 boarders paying £50 per annum, and 20 day boys paying £30 per annum. This would have been a large expense for the Bells, although their sons' education may have been sponsored as it had been at Sydney College. [90]

Among Elizabeth Fry's recommendations for the factory had been the formation of a Ladies' Committee, which she believed was essential for good governance of female convicts. This committee was set up under Governor Darling. Governor Gipps explained in October 1840 that he did not believe this committee would be 'useful', and that the final authority for the factory was now vested in the visiting magistrate. [91]

Perhaps, the governor also believed the pastoral care role of the ladies' committee has been taken over by the Catholic Irish Sisters of Charity who arrived in December 1838, four months after the Bells' return. They were the first religious women to come to Australia, and had been sent to administer to the female convicts.

They visited the factory on 20 January 1839:

> About 800 women and children assembled in the
> yards and corridors to be presented and years later
> [it was] impossible for them to describe the joy and
> gratitude of women as they welcomed the Sisters to
> their wretched abode ... They received our Instructions
> with respect & attention, and before three months
> had elapsed we had the consolation of hearing
> from the Excellency the Lady Gipps, and from the
> Superintendents [sic], that cursing, blasphemy and
> the hitherto daily use of improper language was much
> diminished. [92]

The sisters lived at Parramatta with very few resources, no permanent home and relied on gifts and donations to support them. They walked everywhere and conditions were often unbearable. 'They have been so sadly tormented by the mosquitoes, especially Mrs Cator, and Mrs O'Brien suffered no little. Yesterday was a most oppressive day on account of the heat.' It was the custom at the time to refer to the sisters as 'Mrs'. [93]

In April 1840 they moved into St Mary's Convent (Nunnery) and taught next door at the school (St Patrick's Primary School) which was in the Catholic Church. Governor Gipps gave permission for them to visit the factory. They went to see the women twice daily, from 6 to 7 in the morning and evening, and taught the children at the school during the day. They administered religious instruction to the women and taught them needlecraft (providing them with sewing kits) and singing. The sisters would have been compassionate and may have understood the women better than other staff at the factory.

This was because they were used to the ways of the Irish which were often mistaken, by others, as bad behaviour and indecency. [94]

Parramatta - Church of England School, Catholic Chapel & School. Together with the Nunnery. "Jolly companions every one" — "Toasting hot day was this." W A Miles.

Unfortunately, the presence of the sisters at the factory fuelled the bitterness, which was growing between Protestants and Catholics, over the perceived power being wielded at the factory. In 1836, the *Church Act* had established legal equality for Anglicans, Catholics, Presbyterians, and later Methodists, but had not been able to limit sectarianism. This had increased with an influx of Irish Catholic immigrants and Protestants had tended to combine the words Catholic and Irish. Governor Bourke, in his reorganisation of the factory in 1836, had included a new position of Roman Catholic Chaplain, at the same salary of £50 as the Anglican Chaplain. This enabled Catholic clergy to visit the factory more often and prompted Julia Leach to write that, 'The Roman Catholic Priest is admitted at all hours…' and John Clapham to declare that, 'Popery is at the head of it [factory].' [95]

In addition, Governor Bourke replaced the committee of management with a visiting magistrate which reduced the power of Samuel Marsden, the resident Anglican chaplain at Parramatta. He had been on the previous committee and a constant visitor to the factory. Samuel Marsden died before the Bells returned on 12 May 1838 and Reverend Bobart, Marsden's son-in-law, became the new chaplain of St John's Church and Anglican minister to the factory. [96]

William Westbrooke Burton, Judge of the Supreme Court of NSW, was one of the most vocal critics of what he saw as the growing influence of the Catholic clergy at the factory:

> From two to four or more Priests, and six Sisters of Charity are labouring day and night amongst us. Upon whatever side we look, these holy Brethren and Sisters are seen making their "exits and their entrances," diffusing, in all directions, the subtle poison which lurks under a fair exterior. The Female Factory and the Hospital, are rarely free from their visits. [97]

The Sisters of Charity saw things very differently:

> The presence of the Sisters was a check on the ill-conduct of many of the officials, who had hitherto indulged in certain evil practices. They determined,

therefore, to free themselves from this restraint, and get rid of the Nuns at any cost. Malicious and preposterous stories were circulated…'. [98]

This bitterness extended to the transfer of children from the factory to orphanages. On 28 January 1839, Sarah provided the governor with a list of eleven children, aged three to eight years old, who had arrived on the *Margaret* on 5 January. Governor Gipps noted that the children needed to be sent, 'to the Orphan Schools and Roman Catholic Institution according to the religion of their parents.' Vicar-General of the Catholic Church, William Ullathorne, complained to the colonial secretary that, 'ten boys, nearly all the children of Catholic mothers and baptised in the Catholic Church' had been sent to the Protestant Male Orphan School at Liverpool. Also nineteen girls, thirteen of whom were children of Catholic mothers, had been sent to the Protestant Female Orphan School at Parramatta. He wrote that he had asked Thomas to, 'retain the Catholic girls in the factory' while he sought advice from the governor. He pointed out that Protestant orphan schools were able to take in Catholic children because they had a 'superfluity' of funds, while the Roman Catholic Orphan School could only fund 70 children.

The governor directed Charles Forbes, the new acting visiting magistrate who had just taken over from Pieter Campbell, to investigate the matter. He found only four children had been sent to Protestant orphanages and, when he spoke with two of their mothers (the other two had already been assigned to settlers), 'they begged that their children might be allowed to remain there.' Perhaps these women were pragmatic and realised that the quality of life for their children might be better at Protestant institutions as they were better resourced. [99]

On his arrival in NSW, Governor Gipps' main objectives for the factory were to improve discipline and reduce costs. In relation to discipline, he believed that for the factory to operate as a prison, the women needed to be physically separated into classes, rather than congregating in large rooms with as many as 50 women. Consequently, before leaving England, he sought permission from Lord Glenelg to build separate cells for, at least, third class women. Glenelg approved this expense and requested an early report on the measures. [100]

Governor Gipps commissioned the new cell block soon after his arrival, and it was completed in September 1839. It comprised three floors, with a total of 72 cells: 18 cells on each of the first and second floors, which were light and airy; and 36 cells on the ground floor which had no light, were half the size of the upper cells and were to be used for solitary confinement. Magistrates could now commit women, guilty of secondary offences in the colony, to be imprisoned in these dark cells on bread and water for up to 20 days at a time. There could be no further solitary confinement for these women for another 20 days, and they could be held there for no more than 60 days per year. The visiting magistrate had the authority to send women to these cells for up to 21 days, for breaches of regulations. The matron also had the power to send them to these cells, for up to three days, if they broke the rules of the factory, including assaults, indecent behaviour or idleness.

Once these cells opened, the number of women in solitary confinement escalated, with ten women incarcerated on 7 September 1939 and 51 on 14 September. A new category, Confined by Order of the Matron, had been added to the State of the Female Factory numbers for the *NSW Government Gazette*. It is clear Sarah used her new powers, with four women listed under this category on 14 September and 29 on 7 December 1839. [101]

The governor viewed these cells as, 'a far more efficacious punishment than it had formerly been.' This would have been good news for William Nairn Gray, Commandant/Police Magistrate at Port Macquarie who requested the removal of fifteen female prisoners from the Port Macquarie Female Factory. He claimed, 'they are totally unfit for any services and … never remain longer in their place than fourteen days before they abscond.' The governor agreed that they should be removed and wrote:

> Let Mrs Bell be officially informed that Women who may be sent to the Factory at Parramatta from any other Factory, are to be kept at Parramatta under the strictest possible control and allowed no indulgence whatever, - also that they are to be considered as entirely unfit for assignment. [102]

Governor Gipps was satisfied with the changes that the new cells had brought about. He wrote to Lord Russell, the current Secretary of State for War and the Colonies, that, 'at the present moment, order, cleanliness, perfect obedience and silence may be said to prevail in the Establishment to a degree scarcely surpassed in any Prison in England.'

He may not have been quite so expansive if he had known that Lord Russell's despatch, in which he disapproved strongly of these changes, was already on its way to NSW. Lord Russell had been attempting to alleviate some of the harsh impacts of transportation and end assignment. Consequently, on receiving Governor Gipps' report on the new cells, he asked for a report from prison inspectors, William Crawford and Whitworth Russell. [103]

These inspectors reported that imprisoning women in dark cells was not recognised under any Act relating to the treatment of prisoners and was only to be used as a punishment for aggravated breaches of prison discipline, and then only for a few days. They also revealed that these cells were so small that they were, 'very inadequate … even for a few days' and recommended that all references to 'dark' should be removed from the *An Act to Abolish the Transportation of Female Convicts*. Lord Russell asked Governor Gipps to amend the Act, and that any future plans for prisons, should be approved by the Secretary of State before any works commenced. The Legislative Council of NSW made the necessary amendments to the Act, based on the recommendations of the inspectors. [104]

The governor defended his decision explaining that the larger cells were, 'for the separate confinement of women of notoriously bad conduct, or women who were habitually troublesome in the Factory.' The smaller, dark cells were for women who convicted a fresh offence. He noted sarcastically that the inspectors did not appear to understand the, 'immense masses of Prisoners, which we have to deal with in this Colony, and the intolerable expense which would be occasioned by building a separate, light and airy apartment for each.' There were almost 900 women and 400 children in the factory when he wrote this despatch in October 1841. [105]

The governor's other objective for the factory was to reduce costs. He believed, 'the governor who keeps his government out of debt is the best.' He had been given clear instructions by the British Government before coming to NSW to economise wherever he could, as the Home Government still paid a large amount of the administration costs of NSW, including the costs of feeding, clothing, housing and managing convicts. Consequently, he wanted the women to earn an income for the government which would also ensure they were not idle, causing unrest at the factory. [106]

He proceeded to introduce a series of initiatives to ensure the women had work although, he admitted, that with overcrowding, there would only ever be enough work for about a third of women. His first scheme was to make twine, from New Zealand flax, into nets for fishing or covering fruit trees to prevent birds stealing fruit. The nets did not sell well so this endeavour was discontinued. His next strategy was for the women to produce needlework for sale, supervised by his wife and housekeeper. The only profit was £50 in three months so, when he and his wife left Parramatta for Sydney after their summer break at the beginning of 1839, the sale of needlework was discontinued. Additionally, once new laundries were completed at the factory, women also commenced washing for the military barracks and hospitals at Parramatta, which, although not providing an income, was a saving for the government.

The governor eventually decided that the best course of action was to take in needlework and instructed Sarah to take orders for needlework from government departments and private individuals. She argued against this, claiming that needlework had been tried before at the factory, and had been performed unsatisfactorily with potential for abuse in accounting. She also saw it as an additional responsibility for her. Governor Gipps insisted, so advertisements were placed in the *NSW Government Gazette* notifying the public that needlework could be taken by Mr Bell at the factory, or Mr Rogers at Hyde Park. Completed work would be delivered once it was paid for. The factory also commenced taking in washing for private individuals on the same terms as the provision of needlework. [107]

The Colonist was impressed by what was happening at the factory:

> Formerly the females confined in the Factory were allowed to pass their time in comparative idleness … latterly, however, a new, and a better system has been introduced … Such of the women as can sew are employed in making up shirts, cotton jackets, &c … The change from slothful idleness to cheerful industry, has had a very happy effect upon the females themselves, who have sufficient sense to appreciate the improvement. [108]

An unforeseen outcome of opening the new cells, was that third class women who completed their punishment in these cells were automatically sent to first class on their release. Perhaps this was done as an incentive for good behaviour, although it led to a dramatic increase in the numbers in first class, from 239 women on 17 August 1939, to 367 women on 14 September. This meant that many more women were receiving the first class ration which, with the governor determined to reduce the costs at the factory, could not continue. His solution was to reduce the rations for all first class women. [109]

This reduction must have caused great consternation among the women. Sarah wrote to the governor in May 1840, appealing on behalf of the first class women, that with winter 'settling in' they did not have sufficient energy to finish the large quantity of work. She felt that, if the governor agreed to reinstate the former ration, the women would be able to complete this work. Charles Forbes, the visiting magistrate, supported her request. But the governor did not agree, although he, 'was willing to encourage exertion by giving rewards out of the money earned by the needlework of the women.' [110]

Consequently, in June 1840 two groups of needlewomen were established from the first class women. About 120 of the 'best conducted women' were chosen from first class women who did needlework for the public. They were divided into small groups and, at the end of each week, their work was assessed. Provided it was up to standard, they received one sixth of their earnings in extra tea, sugar, bread, meat or vegetables. The remainder of the women in first class, received no compensation and received the same ration as third class women. [111]

Sarah must have been disappointed by the governor's response although not surprised. In June the previous year, she had written to the governor seeking permission for third class women to wear shoes and stockings, as the weather was becoming colder. She included a statement from Dr Robinson who certified that there had been a, 'considerable increase of disease evidently induced by the sudden & great atmospheric changes.' Sarah noted that the women had been:

> prohibited from wearing shoes and stockings by the regulations of Sir Richard Bourke made in 1836. I am given to understand that they were supplied with them before that date - … they recently get cold in consequence of the sudden change from comfortable clothing in private service to a light dress here. I further beg to recommend the winter issue should be changed from July to June and the Summer issue from January to December.

Female Factory
June 19 1839

Clothing for Female Convicts in 3rd Class

Sir

I do myself the honor to transmit the accompanying certificate from Doctor Robinson relating to the women under punishment in the 3rd class of this establishment who are prohibited from wearing shoes and stockings by the regulations of Sir Richard Bourke made in 1836. I am given to understand they were supplied with them before that date - (The Winter Season only) each year and am of opinion they frequently got cold in consequence of the sudden changes from comfortable clothing in private service to a light dress here.

I further beg to recommend the winter issue should be changed from July to June and the Summer issue from January to December.

I have the honor to be
Sir
your obt sert

S. Bell
Matron

Matron
Female Factory
1 July 1839.

Letter from Sarah Bell to the Colonial Secretary, 19 June 1839. NSWSA: NRS 905, [4/ 2451.3] 39/6925

In fact, during Governor Darling's administration, all the women were permitted to have shoes and stockings but, under Governor Bourke's 1836 regulations, only first and second class women were permitted shoes.

Charles Forbes, the visiting magistrate, agreed with Sarah's request. But the governor refused her request, replying that women could wear shoes and stockings, 'if they have them of their own [it would be] impossible to supply them in any quantity before the present cold.' On the subject of women receiving their winter issue a month early, he replied optimistically that the, 'Weather may be reasonably be expected to be over [soon].' It was the middle of June in Parramatta so it would have been cold and unlikely to become warm anytime soon.

On the return of the Bells in August 1838, there were 623 women and 141 children in the factory, about 100 more women and 20 more children than when they left in February 1838. One reason for this rise in numbers was the continual arrival of female convict ships. Soon after their return, the *John Renwick* landed, followed in 1839 by five female convict ships, the *Margaret, Whitby, Minerva, Planter* and *Mary Ann*. The *Surry* and *Isabella* arrived in early 1840. Finally, the transportation of convicts to NSW ceased in 1840, with the arrival of the last ship, the *Margaret,* which landed in Sydney on 18 August 1840. [112]

In addition to these ships, the *Sophia Jane* landed in Sydney in May 1839, with the remaining 57 convict women and sixteen children from the Female Factory at Moreton Bay which had closed. Five of these women were freed immediately and the remaining women were sent to the factory. Sarah sought advice from the governor on their status:

I shall continue to employ them in the Laundry on First Class rations (where they are at present) or if the entire are to be kept in the third class and their hair cut ... Twelve of them with their children I have placed in the second class'.

Governor Gipps replied that the women, 'should be placed in the 3rd class but their hair <u>not</u> cut.' [113]

The Bells were increasingly concerned with this growing number of women at the factory. In September 1838, Sarah wrote directly to the governor, bypassing the visiting magistrate, to explain that she was unable to find 'situations' for the growing number of women and children in second class. She proposed that the governor could grant tickets-of-leave for country districts for some women who were due for tickets-of-leave but who had, 'punishments on record against them [which normally] debars their obtaining them in the regular way.' She referred to a reference in the *Government Gazette* of 4 October 1837 where 22 women had 'received that indulgence'. She provided the governor with a list of ten women: Bridget Maddin and Caroline Brown per *Numa* (1834), Catherine McGarry, Teresa Lynch, Jane Delehunt, Alice Divine, Mary Crawford per *Andromeda* (1834), Eliza Gardiner and Sarah Bulpin per *Kains* (1831) and Susannah Watson per *Princess Royal* (1829).

The governor immediately sought advice from Pieter Campbell, the visiting magistrate, who was unhappy Sarah had gone directly to the governor. The matron was meant to recommend women for tickets-of-leave to the visiting magistrate, who then referred them to the governor for approval. Campbell claimed Sarah was treating the process as a, 'mere matter of expediency [because] these women and their children are very much in the way'.

He provided the governor with a full report on each of the ten women including their various misdemeanours since they had arrived in NSW and pointed out that:

> their children are all illegitimate (seven of these women being unmarried and the husband of the eighth [Susan Watson] being at Home) … I therefore must hesitate before I can in any way be the means of their receiving the same benefits at the same time with those who have behaved well…

The women did not obtain their tickets-of-leave. [114]

Sarah had more success with a petition from William Snell, the husband of Mary Snell (née O'Conner) per *Mariner* (1825). Mary had been sentenced in January 1839, to fourteen days 'in the cells' for drunkenness, and had lost her ticket-of-leave. Two months later, William, with the support of Nelson Lawson, his employer, wrote to the governor asking him to restore it. Sarah verified that Mary Snell, 'had conducted herself very well while in the Factory' and her ticket-of-leave was restored. [115]

Although the factory was a place of refuge for women, it would have also been a distressing place. Many women had lost their children, their freedom and had to conform to various rules and regulations. They had already endured the dislocation and anguish of leaving their homelands, which may have made them edgy, aggressive, depressed or irrational. Eliza Flowers, alias 'Kesiah Plough', had been convicted of larceny and transported for seven years from Port Adelaide in November 1839. She arrived at the factory, via the Sydney Bench, on 28 December 1839. Five months later, Sarah wrote to the colonial secretary requesting that Eliza be admitted to Tarban Creek Lunatic Hospital, which had opened in 1838. She enclosed a certificate from Dr Kinnear Robertson, Colonial Surgeon at Parramatta. He confirmed that Eliza had been in the factory for some time, and suffered 'under mental derangement, - and [he would] recommend her as a fit object for the Lunatic asylum.' [116]

Tarban Creek Lunatic Asylum. W.A. Miles.

Other women responded to the environment at the factory by continually absconding. Mary Coffey (Coffee) per *Sir Charles Forbes* (1837), came from Tipperary and was a, '…kitchenmaid, 5 feet 1 inch, dark ruddy com., dark brown hair, chestnut eyes, cross scar centre of upper lip, scar right side of upper lip, scar left side of forehead'. She escaped from the factory on 22 August 1839. She was apprehended soon after, but escaped again on 2 October 1839 and 23 May 1840. [117]

Another way a woman could escape from the factory, and gain some sort of freedom, was through marriage. The factory acted as a marriage bureau where free, emancipated or ticket-of-leave men could seek wives. However, like assignment, it was often a lottery for women.

Towards the end of 1838, Sarah received a visit from George Chaplin (Chaplain) who, 'represented himself as a free man and that he had a farm near this town and wished I would recommend him a steady female to whom he might get married'. Sarah asked George for a reference, and he produced a certificate from Mr Hunt of Parramatta, who said George had arrived as an emigrant. Mr Hunt had lent him land and stated that he would support him, until he was self-sufficient. George would have been ushered into a room, while Sarah went to speak with the first class women, in order to gauge their interest in finding a husband. Those women who were interested, would have accompanied Sarah and paraded past George, who had the opportunity to ask questions about their age, if they have ever been married, etc. The women could also ask questions, and in this case may have asked George how many head of cattle or sheep, or what land or houses, he owned. George chose Caroline (or Catherine) Little per *Henry Wellesley* (1835) who was 17 and she accepted his proposal. Once the governor approved the marriage, Sarah would have given George the necessary documents for the clergyman, Reverend Bobart, who married them at St John's Parramatta on 17 November 1838. [118]

Sarah also sought mitigation of some of the women's sentences. Jane Guthery arrived in NSW as a free woman, and on 11 February 1838 was convicted of murdering her baby at Illawarra. As there was no proof of the murder charge, she was found guilty of concealing the birth and sentenced to the factory for two years. A year after her arrival at the factory, Sarah sought a mitigation of her sentence as a 'deserving person' which was granted by Governor Gipps. [119]

Once again the assignment of women from the factory continued to be a problem for the Bells, particularly when settlers tried to shortcut the process. Mary Horn (or Horan) of Sussex Street, Sydney wrote to Sub-Matron Corcoran, asking if she, 'would not be offended in my sending you a little acknowledgement which is enclosed in this note … I hope you sending [sic.] me Phoebe Wilson.' This was seen as a bribe and visiting magistrate, Charles Forbes, decided to give half the money to the Benevolent Society and half to Mrs Corcoran. The governor did question whether a, 'more severe punishment can be inflicted on her.' [120]

An inducement was also offered to Thomas by John Clarke, who asked for two women. Clarke enclosed £1 for 'Postage' and apologised for any further trouble, 'but I have not time [to] visit Parramatta to make a selection.' Although Charles Forbes gave Clarke the benefit of the doubt, saying perhaps he was a stranger in the country, the governor interpreted it as a bribe. He asked for an advertisement to be placed in the *Government Gazette,* stating that the money had been paid to the Benevolent Asylum and that, in future, the name of the person would be published and they would not be permitted convict servants. [121]

The same routine matters continued to consume the Bells' time on their return, with Sarah now handling most issues relating to the women, as well as staffing. Within a month, two turn-keys resigned. Sarah made the surprising recommendation to the governor that, because he had decided that third class women should no longer break stones, the position of the turnkeys who had overseen this work, were no longer required. Instead, she recommended employing an additional clerk in their place, because she contended that there was sufficient work. Pieter Campbell disagreed that the turnkeys should be discharged, yet did agree with the appointment of another clerk. 'I formerly mentioned to the Governor that I do not think Mr Bell competent to perform clerical employment.' Perhaps his advice was a forewarning of what was to come and if he had remained visiting magistrate, the books at the factory may have been scrutinised more thoroughly. Another clerk was not appointed. [122]

The next staffing change was the resignation of midwife Elizabeth Scott and Sarah recommended Eliza Donahue (Elizabeth Donohoe) per *Rosalin Castle* to take her place. She had assisted Elizabeth Scott and Sarah believed, although she was a convict, 'she will suit as well as any free women that can be procured as they only come here for a short time to establish themselves.' [123]

At the end of 1840, Governor Gipps wrote to Lord John Russell, Secretary of State for War and the Colonies, that he had, 'reason to be well satisfied with the conduct and exertions of Mr. and Mrs. Bell [and would] continue to give my unwearied attention to this Establishment.'

He believed overcrowding would be solved now that transportation to NSW had ceased. Unfortunately his prediction did not occur. Five months later, there were 836 women and 190 children still in the factory. To make matters worse, the Home Government was about to make another change of policy which would mean the numbers would continue to climb. This would place greater pressure on all those involved in administering the factory, with dire consequences. [124]

CHAPTER 6.

'Mrs Bell's academy for young ladies at Parramatta':

THE DOWNFALL *of the* BELLS

In April 1841, the Government announced that convicts in the Sydney area could no longer be assigned to settlers. By the end of that year, this decision was expanded to include convicts in the whole colony. Consequently, from the end of 1841, women in the factory could no longer be assigned and were only permitted to leave the factory once they obtained their certificate of freedom, ticket-of-leave or married. Women who were already assigned and lost their tickets-of-leave, because of their misconduct or ill-treatment by their employers, had to return permanently to the factory. Consequently, numbers continued to grow and in July 1842, there were 1,203 women and 263 children - the maximum number ever housed in the factory. [125]

At the same time, as a result of an international economic depression, the British, who had financed rapid expansion in the colony since the late 1830s, commenced to remove their capital from NSW. There was also a severe drought and falling wool prices in the colony, during the late 1830s and early 1840s, which reached its lowest point in 1842. Consequently, settlers were less inclined to employ women and, if they recruited anyone, they preferred to employ free migrant women who were still arriving in large numbers. [126]

With these grim economic conditions, Governor Gipps was even more determined for the women in the factory to earn income for the government. He also believed that work would keep the women occupied, so they had less time to focus on the overcrowded conditions. He instructed Sarah, in February 1841, to commence taking in washing for the public (they were already doing washing for government departments). She was to charge two shillings per dozen for 'ordinary' washing and 'in proportion' for articles which were not 'ordinary' washing. Sarah responded to his request by suggesting the women receive some recompense for this work. She suggested that, after deducting 1/12th from earnings for expenses (starch, soap, etc.), the women could receive 1/6th of the remaining income, in kind. The governor agreed that they could receive some compensation. But he insisted, in his usual miserly way, that 12% (rather than 1/12th) should be deducted for expenses and that the women would receive 1/6th of the remaining income. This meant women obtained less under his scheme. [127]

This increased Sarah's workload. She had already been managing women doing needlework since the beginning of 1839 and organising the washing for government departments. In April 1840, Thomas wrote to Governor Gipps seeking compensation for their extra responsibility, and the work associated with an ever increasing number of women and children at the factory. He wanted an increase in salary but the governor did not grant it, ' in consequence of it being fixed by the Secretary of State'.

Not deterred, Thomas requested, instead, a ration allowance and, 'a commission on the amounts of the money earned since we commenced the work which would be equally as satisfactory as an increase of the Salaries.' Governor Gipps did agree that the Bells should receive a ration allowance, back dated to 1 May 1839 for, 'the great additional trouble occasioned at the Factory by the introduction of needlework and as a mark of my appreciation of Mr. & Mrs. Bells' conduct in the Superintendence of the Establishment.'

Thomas must have been pleased with the governor's support, although Mr Miller at the commissariat office proceeded to offer Thomas a convict ration allowance. Thomas complained and the governor confirmed that the ration, received in kind, should be the same as a colonial surgeon (although in a later note recommended the same ration as a colonial assistant surgeon). After three months, Mr Miller declared that rations could not be back dated to 1 May 1839, as back rations were forbidden by regulation. [128]

It is not clear if the Bells ever received this ration allowance as in May 1843, Governor Gipps claimed in a dispatch to Lord Stanley, who was now Secretary of State for War and the Colonies, that, 'The House Steward and the Matron (Man and wife) have accommodation for themselves and family in the building but no Rations, and a salary between them of £300 a year.'

In the same despatch to Lord Stanley, Governor Gipps proudly reported that the factory had made a net profit. This included £5,288, from needlework and washing for the four years from the beginning of 1839 to the end of 1842, and, in addition, that needlework was being done free of charge for government departments. He added that he had been, 'earnestly solicited by the Steward and Matron', that they should receive a percentage of these earnings. He acknowledged that their workload and responsibility had grown enormously since the introduction of needlework and washing, and they had received no compensation since they returned in August 1838. He felt it was appropriate to approve this extra money because, if the Bells had an interest in the work, it was more likely that the work would be done carefully and would be an incentive to obtain further work. He proposed that the Bells and sub-matron, Mary Corcoran, should receive £264 (5% on the net profit of £5,288), with the Bells receiving 2% each (£211 4s), and Mrs Corcoran 1% (£52 16s). He added that this was not a large amount and would be a reward for three years' labour.

The governor must have been keen for the Bells and Mary Corcoran to receive this extra remuneration, as he wrote a specific despatch highlighting it, rather than embedding the request in his despatch relating to the factory. It is not clear how long the Bells had been lobbying for recompense for their extra responsibilities. They must have known the governor was finally addressing the issue because, in 1846, Thomas referred in his memorial to, 'the additional allowance for which he had been recommended to the Secretary of State in the year 1843.' It appears the Bells never received this allowance, and when circumstances changed at the factory later in 1843, it was no longer relevant. [129]

Why did the governor not attempt to increase the Bells' salaries until this time? He justified increasing Mary Corcoran's salary by £15 to £75 a year in February 1842, because of, 'The great increase of Receipts on account of Needle work and washing seems to me to justify [this], and as the total amount paid for salaries, is considerably below what has been authorised by the Sec. of State (viz £1000 per annum).' [130]

Almost five years had passed since the Bells returned to the factory. It had taken all this time, for the governor to finally acknowledge that they should be compensated for the increased workload. Perhaps, over these years the Bells started to feel overworked and overlooked. They would have been aware that government employees often ran their own businesses, as the public service did not offer many opportunities for promotion.

They may have felt that, 'without prospects of promotion, a little material enterprise was excusable.' [131]

Sarah continued to administer the assignment of women to and from the factory, until assignment was finally abolished at the end of 1841. One of the regulations administering assignment, was that husbands had to collect their wives from the factory, as soon as their sentences expired. Anne Dean per *New Grove* (1835) was confined to the factory for 24 hours on 6 June 1840. Sarah warned Anne's husband, two days later, that he would be charged 2s 6d per day for her support, if he did not collect her. Even after this warning, he still accrued a debt of £2. Caroline Mason (or Williams) per *Sovereign* (1829) had been abandoned by her husband Edward Walton, a blacksmith from Brickfield Hill in Sydney. Consequently, she was sent to the factory on 2nd January 1839 and was discharged on 29 January 1839. Her husband was notified but did not collect her. He accrued a debt and the correspondence, relating to this debt, dragged on for years. [132]

On the other hand, there were some husbands who did want their wives returned to them. James Patchett petitioned the governor for the release of his wife, Anne Patchett per *Sovereign* (1829). Sarah reported that she had been sentenced on 7 August 1841, to fourteen days solitary confinement, with orders not to be returned to Sydney. The petition was refused based on a report from William Miles, Commissioner of Police, who claimed that James was, 'a drunken disorderly character and his wife is as bad as he is.' James Patchett tried again in June 1842, and this time, was supported by Jacob White, from the Sydney Total Abstinence Society and William Macpherson, Collector of Internal Revenue. They claimed that James Patchett was a free man and a carpenter living at Exeter Place, Campbell Street, Sydney since his arrival. He kept a few cows and his wife would take milk for sale and the, 'loss he has sustained from his being deprived of her has consequently been great.' The governor finally recommended that she could be released to her husband on 25 June 1842. [133]

These regulations relating to convict women being assigned from the factory continued to be amended. In 1841, probably foreshadowing the end of assignment, it was mandated that any woman returning from assignment, who had previously been at another female factory, must be kept at the Parramatta Female Factory. The governor had, apparently, informed Thomas of this new regulation, 'verbally'. Catherine Kelly per *Caroline* (1833) had been assigned from the Female Factory at Ballarat to John Forrester of George Street, Sydney. He accused her of a 'transgression' during her assignment, and she was sentenced to third class of the Parramatta Female Factory. Once her sentence expired in June 1841, Forrester wanted her returned. Sarah replied that under the new regulation, Catherine Kelly needed to remain at the Parramatta Female Factory. Forrester wrote to the governor explaining that when she had been assigned to him, he did not know she had been in another female factory and he believed Sarah had overstepped her authority, by rescinding the orders of two magistrates. Sydney Cotton, now visiting magistrate, recommended that another woman should be assigned to Forrester, and Governor Gipps agreed. This must have been an exception because, from April 1841, convicts in the Sydney area could no longer be assigned to settlers. [134]

During 1841, conditions at the factory were becoming even more crowded and women were desperate to leave. Ellen Fitzpatrick per *Margaret* (1840) absconded on 25 July 1841, for the second time, after placing tables on top of each other beside the laundry, 'by which she effected her purpose.' A month later, Ellen Clarke per *Minerva* (1839), and Mary Quin per *Isabella* (1840), escaped via a rope attached to the boundary wall. At the end of that year, Mary Quin absconded again with Ann Murray per *Whitley* (1839) and Caroline Carter per *John Renwick* (1838). It was claimed that, Mrs Corcoran, the sub-matron:

> let the female prisoners into the dormitory from the yard, without counting them. Seeing this, three women managed to secrete themselves in the yard, and it being wet, there was no chance of any of those vigilant guardians of the softer sex, who watch over the safety of their frailer daughters, going out in the pouring rain to look if any were behind. When night came on, and all was quiet, the three runaways broke open the store, and taken out a quantity of rope, made a kind of ladder to the end of which one of these heroines attached her petticoat, filled with stones; this they threw over the top of the walls, and the petticoat catching in the chevaux de frize at the top, they were enabled to scale the wall with little difficulty, and to get clear off. [135]

Ellen Clarke must have been returned to the factory. However, in September 1843, she tried to commit, 'suicide by strangulation in one of the cells, where she had been placed by direction of the Surgeon under the care of the hospital attendants.' Patrick Hill, Colonial Surgeon, explained that she was, 'labouring under great mental depression'. He claimed he would have sent her to the Parramatta Hospital but the deputy inspector general of hospitals had ordered that no female convicts were to be sent to that hospital, because it was so overcrowded. The existing records do not reveal if she was transferred to the Lunatic Asylum at Tarban Creek. Martha Bergin per *Sir Charles Forbes* (1837) had been transferred to this asylum three months earlier, after Sarah said she was unable to look after herself. Sarah provided two surgeons' certificates revealing that Martha had been, 'insane for several months past and subjected to medical treatment in the Factory without benefit'. [136]

In October 1842, the governor visited the factory where there were 1182 women and 283 children. He recalled that the women, 'were in a state of great excitement [and] the peculiar hardship of their condition was, I perceived, perfectly understood by them.' The women were respectful to him, although they made it clear that they had been sentenced to transportation, not imprisonment. They compared their conditions with those of women in Millbank Prison in London who served three, four or five years. These sentences equated to being transported to NSW for seven or fourteen years or for life. In addition, once transported to NSW, they could spend many years in the factory where they endured discipline as severe as Millbank, as well as many discomforts. Then, when their sentences expired, they were only eligible for tickets-of-leave which could be cancelled at any time. [137]

Sister De Lacy, a Sister of Charity, recalled the governor's visit, noting that the women had, 'acted with the utmost forbearance … and they represented to him in the most respectful language their grievances, and called on him to have their wrongs redressed.' She added that the women had mentioned being, 'unjustly deprived for both the quantity & quality of Rations allowed by Government.' [138]

On the basis of the women's accounts during his visit, Governor Gipps decided to appoint a board to look into the state of the factory and to investigate the women's complaints. The board's report recommended improving conditions in the factory by: providing a better diet, as the poor quality of provisions meant some women were suffering from scurvy; reducing the numbers in the factory; and including some 'indulgences' for the women. [139]

On receiving this report, the governor reinstated the first class ration to all first class women, rather than the 120 well behaved women, instigated in 1839. However, he argued the reduced ration should have been sufficient to sustain the women, and blamed the commissariat office (the department for the supply of food and equipment). The commissariat had procured the contract for supplying rations to the factory in 1842, at a very low rate, and there were not sufficient regulations in place to ensure the rations provided were of good quality. [140]

In fact, the governor had been made aware of the poor state of women's rations by Pat Hill, the colonial surgeon, six months earlier, when he complained that the bread was:

> very inferior in quality and not according to the conditions of Contract, which states that the Bread should be made from "sound Colonial meal" … [not] … damaged foreign flour … [containing] … a large admixture of damaged rice or some other unwholesome material … [and consequently many of the women] … are now affected with Bowel Complaints for whom there is not Hospital accommodation.

In response to the surgeon's complaint, the governor asked William Miller, Deputy Commissary-General in NSW, to provide a report on the quality of the bread being supplied to the factory. Miller selected an arbitrator to look into the complaint, which was the process when there was a problem with government contracts. The arbitrator's response was that the bread was wholesome, although badly baked. Governor Gipps was unhappy that contractors were able to have an arbitrator who, he claimed, would:

> in nine times out of ten decide against the Government … [and that] … The question was not, or at least ought not to have been, whether the Bread was sweet, or whether it was well baked - but whether it was agreeable to contract. I have seen the bread, and I will defy any honest man in N. S. Wales to say it was according to Contract.

Later, in a report to Lord Stanley, he justified not having brought the matter to the attention of the Home Government at this time, because he thought it would increase prices for rations. In fact, he was trying to save government money, to the detriment of the women's health. He probably thought his superiors in London might blame the women's poor health on him, particularly when they disovered he had reduced the women's rations. [141]

Governor Gipps had also been having discussions about another matter relating to the factory. William Miller, had alleged that:

> For about two years past, Mr. Bell's expenditure appeared to be inconsistent with any means which he was known to possess; and both he and Mrs Corcoran were at the same time depositing money in the Savings Bank at an extent beyond their Salaries, which caused it to be suspected that they were deriving some improper advantage from their situations.

He informed the governor that he had made several attempts

to find evidence of any malpractice at the factory but at that time he was unable to find proof. [142]

The board's report on the women's conditions in the factory, also recommended reducing the number of women in the factory. The governor decided to provide more tickets-of-leave so women could leave the factory. Notices were placed in the *Government Gazette* explaining that women were available as servants and those interested, should apply to Sarah Bell. In February 1843, even though the numbers were dropping at the factory, the governor introduced a further incentive. An applicant could apply for a woman to be placed in private service, at wages approved by the governor (£8 to £10 per year). The governor described this arrangement as, 'midway between that of an assigned servant and the holder of a Ticket of Leave'. He claimed that by May 1843, 234 women were placed in private service.[143]

These changes did not solve the women's problems. On the evening of 17 February 1843, the women rioted. Gilbert Eliott, now the visiting magistrate, wrote to the governor at 3am the following morning, reporting what had transpired:

> A very serious disturbance which took place at the Factory last night at 6 o'clock when the women were mustered [and] three of them were absent. Mrs Corcoran after considerable time found them concealed upon the top of the roof of the 3rd class sleeping room [and] she ordered them to come down upon which they commenced pelting her with brickbats, a woman named Dempsey had opened the door into the 3rd class sleeping room and let all the women out who commenced throwing everything

they could lay their hands on at Mr Bell and the other persons who were assisting him … They succeeded in getting the women back to their bedrooms and afterwards in putting the three women and Dempsey into the cells at this time. I was sent for and found all the women in the 3rd class on my arrival locked up in the rooms they were yelling dreadfully and behaving in a very riotous manner … [wanting to] … escape or trying to rescue the four women alluded to from the cells. They were then so violent that I sent for the military and Police who shortly after arrived. I used my utmost exertions to try and persuade the women to go quietly to their beds, but they would not listen to me and continued screaming and yelling and began throwing stones & brickbats at the gates of the yard, they broke the gate leading from the 3rd class yard into the first class yard, I then placed military at the different gates and went myself with the Police … [and] … succeeded in getting them into their bedroom after much resistance … The Chief Constable received a severe injury from the blow of an iron bar on the chest and Mrs Corcoran who behaved throughout in a much praiseworthy manner got a cut of an axe on the hand. I have just left the Factory [at] nearly 2 o'clock after having placed sentries on all the gates, the women are still very much excited and I am afraid we shall have great difficulty with them at day light.

The governor visited the factory the next day. He found all was 'tranquil' and that the 30 ringleaders were 'secured'. However, later that day the visiting magistrate provided an update:

The women were quiet all yesterday after your Excellency was there and went to bed in an orderly manner. This morning they made a slight demonstration by yelling and behaving in a disrespectful manner to Mr Bell who immediately sent for me. Mrs Corcoran tells me from what she can learn they are planning another disturbance … I was at the Factory three times today when they were all quiet and they have gone to bed as usual tonight. The cells of the Factory are all full and I have sent twelve women to the cells in the Gaol. They have been behaving in a most riotous manner in the cells. One woman overpowered Mrs Corcoran and got out of her cell and ran to the other cells and tried to open them to release the other women when she was secured. They have passed the word along the cells to try and open the doors by constant hammering with the mops of their tubs and the first woman that gets out is to break the locks of the other cells. They have continued hammering all day and making desperate noise and have broken all the Tubs that have been put into the cells … this evening I made the constables take hold of ten of the worst and tie their hands behind their backs [and] when this was done, the others immediately became very quiet. I am very sorry I have recourse to such measures but with the circumstances I thought I could not do other wise … [144]

A few months later Governor Gipps, in a despatch to Lord Stanley, provided a different account saying that, 'two women were discovered by the sub-matron to have scorched themselves for the purpose of escaping or of endeavouring to escape.'

He estimated that more than 100 women were involved and that:

> A heavy rain fortunately fell soon after the commencement of the fray; and the Women were probably only prevented by it from setting fire to the building. There were at the time 815 Women in the Factory; but only those of one Ward took any part in the riot. Some Women from other Wards and especially those who had Children in the Factory came to the assistance of the Sub-Matron. [145]

The Australian also weighed in, reporting that Thomas had discovered three women were missing. He found them trying to escape through the roof and, on putting them in cells, the other prisoners:

> commenced the most violent abuse ... and in fact, had Mr. Bell not speedily withdrawn, his life would have been endangered ... Too much praise cannot be awarded to all the authorities (as well as to Mr. Bell), whose promptness and determination quelled this most desperate riot ... [146]

Instructions were immediately given to undertake repairs, and workers proceeded to strengthen any doors that were insecure by sheeting them over with hardwood and fitting stronger hinges. The governor informed William Miles, Superintendent of Sydney Police, that in future, if Mr Eliott needed assistance at the factory, he was to provide support. [147]

Gilbert Eliott had been appointed visiting magistrate in June 1842, after Pieter Campbell, who had been acting colonial treasurer, left the colony. This provided stability to the Parramatta magistracy which had been lacking for many years.

He appears to have taken on a greater role at the factory, particularly after the riot in February 1843. In April he reported to the governor on:

> the good conduct and regular attendance of all the inferior officers of the Establishment during the month of March 1843. The behaviour of the Prisoners for the greater part of the same period has been generally good, and the rations with one or two exceptions have been of a good quality. [148]

However, four months later there were more problems at the factory. On 8 August 1843, there was an altercation between Sarah and Mary Corcoran, the sub-matron. Mary had been a housemaid in Waterford, Ireland and was convicted of stealing coal. She had received a sentence of transportation for seven years and arrived in Sydney per *Hooghley* (1831). She was assigned to various settlers over the next five years. But she was returned to the factory for several misdemeanours, including drunkenness, absence without leave, absconding, robbery and insolence. Finally, in 1836, approval was granted for her to remain permanently in the factory. [149]

Sarah appears to have advocated for Mary. In August 1837, she recommended that Mary receive a gratuity for guarding clothes that needed to be laundered as, 'I have found very great inconvenience in not having a secure place for the Clothes which leave them liable to be stolen by the women.' This request was approved and, just over a year later, Mary received her certificate of freedom. In January 1839, Sarah sought permission for her to be a turnkey which was endorsed by Pieter Campbell. He stated that, 'This woman's services have always been valuable - and I think her quite equal to the office of Turnkey'. A year later she was appointed sub-matron. [150]

Perhaps, over the years, there was increasing conflict between her and the Bells. She may have been influenced by her friendship with Anne Edgeley per *Margaret* (1837), who became a turnkey and overseer of the laundry at the factory. When Anne Edgeley died in April 1844, Mary erected an expensive tombstone for her. [151]

On 9 August 1843, Sarah wrote to Gilbert Eliott accusing Mary of disorderly conduct and insubordination. She believed that she could no longer ignore the, 'outrageous and extraordinary conduct of Mrs Corcoran' and that in reporting her, 'I earnestly trust you will believe, that I am not actuated by any personal feeling, but, simply by the desire to present the order, regularity and propriety which should characterize an Establishment of this description.' Sarah claimed that:

> For a length of time it has been apparent to me, that the Sub-matron instead of yielding to me that assistance which it is her duty to do, has sought every opportunity to place impediments in my path; and in this it grieves me to say that she has been but too successful, and has compelled me to feel that the contraction rather than the proper extension of my authority has been her sole aim, and, though I have hitherto borne it uncomplainingly in the hope that her better feeling and sense of reflection would induce an alteration in her conduct, yet, I find that my consideration is entirely misinterpreted, and I therefore feel myself imperatively called upon to place this complaint before you, and more particularly a relation of the occurrences of last night.

Sarah reported that the previous evening she had left the factory, to pick up her son and daughter, and took with her, 'Female Servants in my employ [who] have conducted themselves very creditably [so] I felt justified in allowing them to walk a short distance with myself.'

They met Mary and Anne Edgeley returning from town in an 'intoxicated state'. Mary was very insolent and proceeded to count the women accompanying Sarah. On Sarah's return to the factory, Mary met her, and the women who had accompanied her, at the gate. Suddenly she struck Ellen Chambers, one of the servants, on the eye and took her coat. When Sarah asked her to return the coat, she claimed Mary defied her authority. She behaved so violently that Sarah was compelled to seek refuge in her own apartments, fearing every moment that Mary would make a forcible attack upon her. Mary then walked up and down the yard for about an hour, 'uttering the most scandalous assertions and threats' and waking the women in the factory. At 10.30pm, Mary sent the gate keeper to seek assistance from the visiting magistrate to, 'quell a disturbance which she alone had incited and which was solely acted by herself.' Sarah wrote that she could not remain at the factory unless the governor controlled Mrs Corcoran's behaviour. [152]

The governor immediately reconvened the board, which had considered the factory women's complaints, in order to investigate Sarah and Mary Corcoran's accusations. The latter provided a written statement to Gilbert Eliott on 21 August 1843.

At the hearing of the board, Sarah reiterated her grievances and cited many other occasions when Mary had been abusive to her, and incited the prisoners to be insubordinate. Thomas supported her by saying that Mrs Corcoran had often been drunk and, on the day in question, Sarah had gone to collect her children from Mr Allan's place accompanied by five of her servants. Later, he heard a commotion at the gate and Mrs Corcoran was abusing his wife and striking a servant. He deduced that she was obstructing his wife. He believed she was discrediting them both, so she could take on administration of the factory. [153]

The board summoned a number of convict women, and some men who worked at the factory, as witnesses. The first witnesses were the servants who had accompanied Sarah. Ellen Chambers per *Princess Charlotte* (1827) was employed by Sarah to do needlework. She confirmed the events, as described by Sarah in her letter to Gilbert Eliott, adding that the blow on her face gave her a black eye. Mrs Corcoran continued for two hours and, 'roared out that she would have Mr Bell in double irons or send him to Hell.' [154]

Eliza Taylor per *Isabella (1840)*, employed as a nurse in the hospital, agreed saying she heard Mrs Corcoran say, 'publickly in the Factory that she would have Mr Bell in Irons or in Hell.' Mary Ann Milton per *John Renwick (1838)* confirmed Ellen Chambers' evidence, adding that she saw Mrs Corcoran strike Ellen. She added that she was very tipsy and, 'must have lost her senses to act as she then did.' Rose Hughes per *Planter* (1838), employed as a house servant by Mrs Bell, stated that, 'Mrs Corcoran threatened to strip them naked and place them in the Cells and, in consequence, they begged of Mr Bell to allow them to remain on his premises all night which they did.' [155]

Mrs Corcoran was then called for questioning and denied that she was 'in Liquor'. She claimed her 'intemperance' with Mrs Bell and the other women was necessary, to preserve the 'regularity' of the factory. Edward New, from Parramatta, was the next witness and claimed that Mrs Corcoran was at his house that night.

She had only had one glass of brandy before leaving with Mrs Edgeley between 8 and 9pm. Mrs Fox and Eliza Kelly, who also resided in Parramatta, had met Mary Corcoran and Anne Edgeley, as they returned to the factory that night and stated that, 'they were both quite sober'. Emily Richardson per *Minerva* (1839) maintained that she had never seen Mrs Corcoran 'the worse of Liquor', and had actually heard Mrs Corcoran check the women, when they spoke disrespectfully to Mrs Bell. Charity Nott, the turnkey (gaoler) of the bells, who slept in the factory hospital, claimed that Mrs Corcoran had been sober when she arrived at the factory soon after 9pm on that night.

The board then considered Mary Corcoran's statement. She listed thirteen charges against the Bells for fraud and breach of trust. She accused Thomas of drawing rations for nearly 100 more children than were in the factory and that, when she pointed out the error, he responded by gradually reducing the numbers of children reported to the *Government Gazette*. She also accused him of drawing more soap than was needed for the factory hospital, and when the surgeon objected to this amount of soap, Thomas tried to persuade her to destroy the surplus to save, 'as he said, himself and family from ruin.' She claimed that she could prove that women in the factory never received their permitted ration of meal. Sarah also used six of the best needlework women to do her own needlework, 'putting no doubt the money in her own pocket.' She contended that, after she reported the Bells, the books, to which only she and the Bells had access, were torn up. The Bells had also approached Reverend Coffee, the Catholic Priest, asking him to try to persuade her to retract her statement. [156]

The board's final report was sent to Governor Gipps on 5 September 1843. It concluded that it, 'appears extremely probable that Mrs Corcoran on the night alluded to, conducted herself as alleged in the charge.' The animosity between the Bells and Mrs Corcoran would make it impossible for all of them to continue to administer the factory. It seemed the board took the claims by Mrs Corcoran against the Bells seriously, and they were suspended immediately, 'with the view of having them (or some of them) indicted for conspiring with the Contractor to defraud the Government.' [157]

The governor submitted this report to the Attorney-General, John Hubert Plunkett, with instructions that the Bells, Mary Corcoran and John Hamilton, the contractor providing provisions to the factory, should appear before the bench of magistrates at Parramatta to answer the charges. The governor noted that Sarah was not to be proceeded against, 'unless in the course of the proceedings it should appear distinctly that she acted in any case altogether independently and free from the control of her husband.' [158]

The Bells left the factory under a cloud of suspicion, in September 1843. The numbers in the factory had dropped to 505 women and 128 children. The convict women would have been aware of the accusations made by Mary Corcoran against the Bells, so they may have been glad to see them leave. Perhaps they expressed their delight on the day of their departure. It appears the Bells remained living somewhere in the area, as any later correspondence includes 'Parramatta' as their address. [159]

The two reports by the board of inquiry had identified that there were problems with the quality and quantity of food being provided to women in the factory. Mr Trevelyan, Secretary of the Treasury in Britain, highlighted that officers of the commissariat in NSW should have ensured that appropriate supplies of food were being provided, according to all relevant contracts. They should also have made sure and that those receiving these supplies for distribution to the women were carrying out their duties diligently. He declared that frequent inspections of convict establishments should be made by relevant officers. Although Governor Gipps had reinstated the first class ration to all first class women, he still maintained that the reduced ration should have been sufficient if it had been of 'sound quality'. In a veiled criticism of the governor, Mr Trevelyan wrote that, 'any description of Ration, which may really be required to preserve the health of the Prisoners, ought to be given.' [160]

Who was to blame for this parlous set of circumstances at the factory? Was it Governor Gipps when he reduced the first class ration for all first class women, expect 120 of the 'best conducted women' and then only as a reward for good work? Was it the commissariat office for agreeing to the supply of rations at too low a rate, therefore ensuring the food would be of poor quality? Were the procession of acting magistrates not checking the books at the factory diligently? Did Thomas and Sarah Bell take matters into their own hands and undertake dishonest activities, in order to make the extra income they believed they were entitled to?

It is highly likely it was all of the above and it was the women at the Parramatta Female Factory who suffered.

CHAPTER 7.

'I had hard and disagreeable work':

THE CASE AGAINST THOMAS BELL
and **JOHN HAMILTON**

On the morning of 6 October 1843, Thomas Bell, John Hamilton and Mary Corcoran arrived at the courthouse in Parramatta. They had been summoned, in order to determine whether there was sufficient evidence to prove the charges of embezzlement and conspiracy. If it was found that there was sufficient evidence, they would be 'committed' (transferred) to stand trial in the Supreme Court in Sydney.

Built in 1837, the courthouse was an imposing stone building on the corner of Church and George Streets, designed by Mortimer Lewis, the colonial architect. Apart from serving as a courthouse, it provided a venue for political meetings and church services, and also served as the police station and lock-up.

Gilbert Eliott, as the police magistrate at Parramatta, should have heard the case. However, as visiting magistrate at the factory, he had a conflict of interest. Consequently, the accused appeared before three justices of the peace, Dr Mathew Anderson, John Blaxland and Captain Moffat, although Captain Moffatt is listed as appearing only on the first day. [161]

Thomas Callaghan, who had been acting as a Crown prosecutor for the government since 1841, conducted the prosecution's case.

Parramatta. Church, Chapel Court House - accommodation for the best of
Saints and the worst of Sinners. W A Miles.

He wrote in his diary that, 'I had hard and disagreeable work ...
for five days and for this I received 22 Guineas.' George Robert
Nichols acted for Thomas and John Hamilton. He was the son of
a convict and opened his practice in 1833, after being admitted as
the first native-born Australian solicitor. In the late 1830s, he had
purchased and became editor of *The Australian*, where he advocated
self-government and denounced transportation. By 1842, he had
become insolvent and the defence of Thomas and John Hamilton
may have helped to salvage his financial affairs. Mr Carrington
acted for Mary Corcoran.[162]

Callaghan opened the case for the Crown, but immediately
Nichols, for the defence, objected to the way Gilbert Eliott had

issued the original summons, 'on so grave a charge as felony, unsupported by affidavit.' Callaghan immediately reproached Nichols, saying that his objection was pedantic but that if he persisted, Callaghan would ensure that another warrant was prepared for the arrest of the prisoners.

Thomas Callaghan

Consequently the court was adjourned. What followed was a bizarre scene. John Ryan, chief constable of Parramatta, armed with warrants, rearrested Thomas Bell in the courthouse yard, John Hamilton on the footpath in George Street, and Mary Corcoran in the police office (located within the courthouse). The court reconvened and, once the charges were read, the case was adjourned for the rest of the day. [163]

Sarah Bell was not present on the first day of the proceedings, even though she must have had the same charges laid against her. She was there on the second day, and Callaghan questioned whether she needed to be present, probably thinking he was unlikely to establish a case against her. This was because she was married and the law saw her as being under the protection of her husband, with no separate legal existence. Nichols, for the defence, argued that she needed to be present, because it was a criminal prosecution and, 'the investigation must be taken in the presence of all arraigned [accused].' [164]

George R. Nichols

As the day's proceedings got underway, Callaghan informed the bench that the prosecution was withdrawing all charges against Mary Corcoran, and she was to be a witness for the prosecution. Once she was in the witness stand, Callaghan asked her when she had first met the Bells. She replied that she had encountered them during their first administration of the factory when, 'Mr Bell … held all offices [and] he was acting in the same capacity as the Matron.'

She was then questioned by Mr Nichols, for the defence. She said that she had always had a:

> good feeling towards Mr Bell and his family …
> [although she did notice] … on their first coming
> to the Factory, Mr and Mrs Bell seemed to live in
> humble circumstances but afterwards they lived in a
> far superior style.

She added that she had only reported the Bells to 'protect herself and ease her conscience.'

Callaghan proceeded to address the crux of the prosecution's case, by asking her about the numbers of women and children in the factory, provided each week to be included in the *Government Gazette*. She replied that, when she was in the factory office on 14 September 1841, she had noticed that the number of children listed under the State of the Female Factory in the *Government Gazette* of 13 September 1841, did not correspond with the actual number in the factory. In fact, the number included 70 or 80 more children than were actually in the factory. According to her, when she told Mr Bell of this discrepancy, he asked her to tell John Johnson, the clerk, that she had made an error and not reported it for fear of Mr Bell's reaction. She declined to do this as that was a lie.

She thought the discrepancy was a mistake, and told Mr Bell he should tell the governor immediately. She claimed that later, Mr Bell had told Johnson to, 'take them [number of children reported in the *Gazette*] off by degrees' which was done.

The Crown prosecutor continued this line of questioning asking her about whose role it was to muster (count) the women and children. She replied that she and Mr Bell did it, although she did not see it as her job. She explained that after the women and children were counted, she and Mr Bell recorded the numbers on dockets. Callaghan presented 40 of these dockets, for the period 30 August to 8 October 1841, to the court. Mrs Corcoran confirmed the numbers on these dockets were in her handwriting, except those from 15 to 23 September 1841. She explained that these dockets had been left blank, so the numbers could be adjusted (reduced) 'by degrees', presumably by John Johnson. It appears this was done. The *New South Wales Government Gazette* recorded that on 14 September 1841, 380 children and 895 women were in the factory. Seven days later on 21 September 1841, there were 333 children and 892 women. In one week 47 fewer children were recorded, while the number of women remained stable. [165]

The prosecution then called John Johnson to the stand. He had kept the books at the factory from June 1839 till October 1842. Under questioning, he explained that one of his jobs was to record the numbers of women and children listed on these dockets. This record was then signed by Mr Bell and provided to the commissariat department and the *Government Gazette*. Callaghan presented Johnson with the same set of dockets that he had been shown Mrs Corcoran. According to Johnson's testimony, the erasure on the docket of 13 September may have been due to a mistake made by Mrs Corcoran, when she counted children in the factory. Mr Bell had mentioned this error to him, and he had thought it strange that she could have made such a large mistake. Mr Bell appeared annoyed about it. He told Johnson that the best way to rectify the error, was gradually to reduce the numbers of children provided in the monthly returns, so the discrepancy would not be noticed. This was done.

Callaghan asked Mrs Corcoran to return to the stand. He commenced questioning her about food rations, and how they were provided to the women and children in the factory. Mrs Corcoran claimed that she had occasionally acted as storekeeper at the factory, and that she and Mr Bell were the only ones who handled the rations. She alleged that after the 'row' some entries had been removed from a receipt book, which was kept in the provisions store. Only she and Mr Bell had the key to this store.

In addition, she claimed that Mrs Bell had asked her while, 'Mr Bell and Miss Bell [Mary Isabella Bell] were present', to say that she [Mary Corcoran] had given out the extra bread which had been ordered for the inflated number of children. She also claimed that Sarah had said if she didn't say this, ' herself [Sarah] and the children would be destroyed.' According to her testimony, Mary Corcoran declined to do this. Later during the court case, Nicholas Coffey, Catholic Chaplain at the Factory, disclosed that during the previous enquiry by the board, Mr Bell had asked him if Mrs Corcoran had said anything 'injurious' about him (Thomas). The Reverend replied that she had not and Mr Bell urged him to tell Mrs Corcoran he'd be ruined if she did. Reverend Coffey told Mrs Corcoran to, 'do justice to the government.'

John Johnson was also questioned about the rations. He claimed that Mr Bell rarely, if ever, handled them and that Mrs Corcoran ordered the bread and meal, and generally, 'seemed to have the management of the store'. The bench immediately queried this statement, stating that this work was surely part of the storekeeper's role. Under further examination by Callaghan about the ordering process, Johnson alleged that no regular requisitions were made for bread, and that loaves were ordered verbally or, sometimes, with a docket.

The next witnesses were two subcontractors who supplied provisions to the factory. Thomas O'Neale from Parramatta had supplied the factory with milk from 1838 to 1842. He claimed he could not guarantee the quantity of milk supplied, as his memory was hazy, and he kept no records during that time. Equally vague was William Peisley, a butcher in Parramatta, who supplied meat to the factory from 1842 to 1843. Apparently, he was frequently away and seldom saw what meat was actually provided to the factory.

At this stage Callaghan discharged Sarah. *The Australian* reported that, 'he was not satisfied ... that he would be able to establish a sufficient case against Mrs. Bell to make her a party' in the case.

The prosecution's next line of questioning, was to try and establish if the children actually received any extra rations. Jane Edge per *John Renwick* (1838), who was in charge of children attending school at the factory, was called to the stand. She explained that she collected the children's rations from Mrs Corcoran, and was sure that the children were not provided with more food than they were permitted. She added that sometimes, 'Mrs. Corcoran of her own goodness gave them some ... "plush", such as fruit, meat or bread, from her own table'. [166]

The court adjourned for the weekend and reconvened on 9 October. Mary Corcoran was once again called to the stand to answer questions about how food rations were allocated. She explained that convict women were issued with a specific amount of food daily (measured in pounds and ounces), depending on whether they were in first, second or third class. Mrs Corcoran claimed that the maize meal (used to make hominy, a porridge) was never weighed, until Mr Eliott and Dr Hill visited the factory about 7 or 8 August 1843 (after the row), and told her to weigh it. If her claim about the maize meal not being weighed was true, it is not clear how the women could have received their allocated rations.

The next witnesses were two cooks at the factory, Anne Sherwin and Lucy Martin, who were asked about the quantity of maize meal used in the kitchen. Anne Sherwin per *Southworth* (1832) had been a cook for four months. She testified that during her first two months, the meal had not been weighed, and she had received half the quantity. The last two months, when the meal was being weighed, there was enough to provide double the quantity of hominy to the women and children. Lucy Martin claimed that Mr Bell frequently entered the kitchen and instructed her to use less meal. He explained that he was in debt to the government, and that if she continued to use substantial amounts of meal, it would ruin him and his family. According to her testimony, he then threatened her saying if she didn't comply, he would put her 'into a top [gaol] cell.' [167]

The following day, Callaghan focused on Mary Corcoran's accusation that large amounts of soap had been purchased by Thomas for the factory. Under questioning, Mrs Corcoran claimed that in early 1843, she received large deliveries of soap and that later that year Mr Bell asked her to destroy some of these supplies. The next witness, Pat Hill the doctor at the factory hospital, explained that after his appointment as surgeon in January 1841, about 60 pounds of soap was being ordered each month, for the hospital. When he queried this amount, Mr Bell said it was necessary. Dr Hill permitted its purchase until August 1843, when he declined to include soap in his account. It was then ordered under the factory account and no more than 20 pounds were ordered per month.

It appears that Callaghan was attempting to establish that large amounts of soap were being bought through the hospital account but much of it was being used in the factory.

Gilbert Eliott, the visiting magistrate, was called to the stand to clarify Thomas' role as factory storekeeper. Eliott outlined the storekeeper's duties: to muster the women and children each morning; to check the matron's numbers from her muster the previous evening; to determine the quantity of rations needed based on this number; and to make requisitions for the rations. It was also his duty to receive the supplies from contractors, and to provide receipts for these supplies.

Eliott then drew on evidence that John Hamilton had provided at the board of enquiry in August 1843, which showed how poorly the books were kept at the factory. According to Hamilton, Thomas' requisitions for factory rations were sometimes done by chits, and sometimes verbally. Hamilton revealed, at that enquiry, that he kept no books recording the supply of these rations, and simply listed them on sheets of paper which were destroyed at the end of each month. Hamilton reported that he kept a running account and settled every month with Thomas, who generally owed him money. It is not clear from the transcript why Thomas would owe him money.

The court adjourned until 14 October when the Crown called two more witnesses, Commissary Goodsir, from the commissariat department, and Henry Johnson, from Hughes & Hosking who employed John Hamilton as their agent to supply provisions to the factory.

Commissary Goodsir commenced by explaining that Thomas provided the commissariat with certified monthly returns for the number of women and children in the factory. Thomas also informed John Hamilton of rations required each day for the factory, based on these numbers and the scale of government rations for different classes of women. Hamilton then purchased these rations—such as milk, maize meal, etc.—from subcontractors, at prices set by contracts they had signed previously with the commissariat. Once Thomas certified the receipt of these goods, John Hamilton submitted cash vouchers to the commissariat which forwarded payment to Hughes and Hosking.

Henry Johnson, from Hughes and Hosking, then took the stand and explained that it was his role to check the value of the vouchers and pay their agent, John Hamilton, who then paid the subcontractors for the goods. [168]

Once all witnesses had appeared, Callaghan proceeded to close the Crown's case. He expressed surprise that Nichols, acting for the defence, had declined to provide a closing statement. However, he, 'deemed it his duty to say a few words as to the course he considered it the duty of the court to pursue.' He believed that he:

> had distinctly proved five charges against Mr Bell,
> and four against Mr Hamilton, of a criminal nature,
> upon all or any of which the defendants might be

committed. To get rid of these charges it would be for the defendants to prove that the quantities charged for were really drawn and required and that the rations so charged for had been supplied.

Callaghan's opinion was that the evidence demonstrated that 80 to 100 extra children were added to the factory's true number. When Mr Bell's attention was drawn to this discrepancy, he, 'recklessly went on despite all remonstrance', continuing to conceal these circumstances, by forging the factory numbers. Callaghan concluded that he was in, 'no doubt but that a fraudulent arrangement had been made between the parties, and that they had both been privy to the frauds practised on the Crown.'

The bench committed Thomas Bell and John Hamilton to stand trial for fraud and embezzlement in the Supreme Court at its next sitting in January 1844. They were each released on bail of £200 and sureties of £100.

It appears there was a strong case against Thomas Bell and John Hamilton. However, the credibility of the main witness, Mary Corcoran, is questionable. In the first five years in the colony, she had recorded an extensive number of misdemeanours while assigned to settlers. In 1836, it was decided that she should no longer be assigned and would remain permanently in the factory and was eventually promoted to sub-matron. Interestingly, on a sub-matron's salary, she was able to accumulate enough funds by October 1845 to own four houses in Parramatta. Was she also involved in the fraud that was taking place at the factory? She eventually assigned the income from these homes to support the Sisters of Charity while they were in Parramatta. [169]

The result of this hearing must have been a huge blow for the Bells as they now faced an impending trial. Did Sarah believe that her husband was guilty? Had she been cooperating with him, or was she completely unaware of what appeared to have taken place at the factory?

The Bells had barely two weeks after this hearing to prepare for a very different event. On 30 October 1843, their daughter Mary Isabella married John Macdonald, of the ordnance office. The ceremony took place at St Johns Church, Parramatta, presided over by Reverend Bobart. [170]

CHAPTER 8.

'The unfathomable factory case':

REGINA V BELL *and* **HAMILTON**

Regina (Crown) V Bell and Hamilton was listed for a hearing in the Supreme Court on 27 January 1844. Thomas may have taken a boat from Parramatta that morning, and then walked from Sydney Cove to the new Darlinghurst courthouse. Sessions of the Supreme Court had been held there since 1842, despite the building being unfinished.

As he reached the courthouse, he would have seen the scale and grandeur of this old colonial style Grecian public building and walked through the imposing Doric columns to the court room which was, 'a light, airy and commodious place'. [171]

Everyone in the court room would have stood when the three judges entered: Chief Justice, Sir James Dowling, and presiding judges, William Westbrooke Burton and Alfred Stephen. The case for the prosecution was led by Attorney General, John Hubert Plunkett, who had arrived in NSW a month after the Bells to take up the position of solicitor general. In 1836, he was appointed attorney general. At this time the attorney general took on the prosecution of many criminal trials which, today, would be carried out by prosecutors in the office of the director of prosecutions. Plunkett had an outstanding legal career which included prosecuting those responsible for the murder of 28 Aboriginal men and women at Myell Creek in 1838.

Bell and Hamilton were represented by the formidable barrister Richard Windeyer assisted by Archibald Michie. He had been in NSW for about ten years, was well respected and had built a considerable practice. He was the leading counsel for the defendants in the *Bank of Australasia V the Bank of Australia* case and when it was over, he was lauded:

Judge John Hubert Plunkett

For learned research, and subtle reasoning, and adroit use of circumstance, and occasional bursts of true eloquence, and powerful appeal to the understandings of the jury ... we have no hesitation in believing that at that bar it had never been surpassed.[172]

Richard Windeyer

Plunkett commenced the proceedings by stating that Thomas Bell and John Hamilton, and perhaps others yet to be identified, had conspired to defraud the Queen of 'certain sums'. Windeyer responded by entering a plea of not guilty and requesting a copy of the 'very long and special' information file for the case. Immediately, the attorney general applied to have the trial adjourned because the case could not proceed without certain alleged 'false returns' which had been sent to England with no duplicates retained in Sydney. [173]

This was the beginning of many adjournments of this case. It was listed for the April and July 1844 sittings of the Supreme Court and, on both occasions, the attorney general sought further adjournments. At the July sitting, Windeyer opposed the application. His argument was remarkably prescient, saying that it was unfair to the defendants because:

> their witnesses might become dispersed all over the
> world …[and] … the evidence in their favour might
> be lost to them there being no law that could compel
> … [witnesses]… to remain in the Colony.

However, the case was adjourned for almost a year to April 1845. [174]

Sir Archibald Michie

This must have been a very stressful period for the Bells whose reputations would have been severely damaged. In February 1845, Sarah, probably instructed by Windeyer who would have been keen to secure witnesses for the defence, wrote to Governor Gipps' private secretary, Henry Parker. She asked that her husband be allowed to select some of the women from the factory to give evidence for her husband:

> in consequence of the very long time that has elapsed,
> since its [trial] commencement, those women that
> could then have assisted in it, are dispersed through
> the country, so that their attendance cannot be
> procured. I hope the unpleasant position Mr Bell
> is placed in will plead my apology for troubling his
> Excellency on the occasion. [175]

On the evidence of the remaining records, it is not clear whether this request was granted, although there were a number of women from the factory listed as witnesses in the trial.

The original documents finally arrived in NSW in January 1845 and then, 'some 110 brief sheets, about 80 folios' had to be copied. The defendants finally appeared in court on 10 April 1845 but, again, the case was adjourned several times because:

> the clerk who had been employed in copying it, one of
> the best copyists they had, copied about sixty folios a
> day. More than one clerk could not be employed as the
> information was a record of the Court and there was
> not authority to divide the string which connected it;
> beside there was not sufficient clerical strength in the
> department. [176]

The Examiner highlighted the, 'strange mode in which the proceedings in the case of the *Queen v. Bell and Hamilton* have been conducted'. It had taken over two years to come to court which caused enormous expense for the defendants. [177]

Finally the trial commenced on 7 October 1845. Chief Justice, Alfred Stephen, was the presiding judge after he had been appointed chief justice on the death of Justice Dowling in September 1844. He was assisted by Justice Dickinson. The prosecution was once again represented by Attorney-General, John Plunkett, and the defence by Richard Windeyer, assisted by Archibald Michie. Michie was a part-time journalist and, in 1855, was a defence lawyer for the Eureka Stockade prisoners. [178]

The jury of twelve men (women were not permitted) were sworn in. The foreman was William Cox who was warden at the Windsor District Council. The other eleven men were John Betts, J.B. Bettington, Edmond Burke, Josiah A. Betts, John Betts, Robert B. Dulhunty, Leslie Duguid, W. S. Deloitte, Robert Crawford, Thomas Cowlishaw and William Dawes (original article lists two John Betts). In order to qualify to be on a jury, men had to hold a personal estate of at least £300, or an income from land of at least £30 per annum, and not have committed a serious crime. [179]

The case was then adjourned to the next day when the attorney general commenced the proceedings. He alleged that Thomas Bell and John Hamilton had, 'unlawfully, wickedly, falsely, fraudulently and deceitfully, contriving and intending to cheat and defraud our said Lady the Queen of her monies with force and arms.'

He laid out nineteen charges against the defendants explaining that the large number of charges were because:

> Legal technicality required that there should be special allegations as to the persons, who were the Government contractors for each year, and this circumstance tended to lengthen the information very much as the Contract and Contractors for each were different. [180]

More than 30 witnesses were listed to be examined on behalf of the Crown. They included owners of some of the businesses which had provided rations to the factory, including Edward New a butcher who had provided meat, and James and William Byrnes who supplied flour. John Hughes and John Hosking from Hughes and Hosking, who had employed John Hamilton as their agent, were also listed, as were Stephen Owen, Deputy Assistant Commissary General and two commissariat clerks, Alfred Salway and James Charles Rudston Wood. Captain Maclean, Superintendent of Convicts and John Ryan, Chief Constable of Parramatta were to provide evidence, as was Gilbert Eliott. Witnesses who worked at the factory were Mary Corcoran, as well as John Johnson and Alexander Cameron, who had been the clerks at the factory, Jane Edge, who looked after the children in the factory, and Caroline James, a laundress.

Three of the witnesses were unable to be present. Instead Andrew Kell, Robert Miller and E Courtney provided sworn statements. Andrew Kell was a shopkeeper in Parramatta and had provided supplies from his store to the factory for two years from 1842. In his statement, he described an orderly purchasing process, whereby Thomas generally sent a signed requisition for the daily supplies, receipts were provided on delivery of goods and orders were put on file and entered into a book.

The other two sworn statements provided a completely different story. Robert Miller, from Robert Miller and Co., who had been in partnership with John Hamilton, stated that:

> the quantities charged for were not supplied to the Factory...[and]...I never remember one single month of the whole period before mentioned when the whole amount of bread was fully drawn according to what was charged for.

He also recalled frequent conversations he had with John Hamilton who said, 'This is a good month for Bell. He will make a good thing of it this month'. Hamilton had determined that Thomas Bell would have received between £30 to £40 per month, as his share of the undrawn provisions.

The next sworn testimony was from E Courtney, an accountant with the Bank of Australasia. He provided a statement alleging that John Hamilton had told him that 'Bell's situation' was worth about £600 a year to him (Hamilton) and that he preferred the factory contract to any other. He also claimed that during a recent meeting of creditors of Robert Miller & Co., Hamilton admitted that there had been no records of supplies and that the only records of the transactions were strips of paper placed on file, which were destroyed at the end of the month. Courtney recounted that about the end of 1839, or the beginning of 1840:

> when provisions were very high and consequently more money to be divided between H & B, Hamilton related to me that Bell was making too expensive an appearance, Keeping a carriage &c; and that it would be much more prudent for him not to do so, as it might open the eyes of Government as to how he got money. [181]

The Supreme Court sat from 8 to 18 October 1845. The proceedings were not reported because *The Australian* declared that as, 'a principle of justice, we forbear publishing the evidence till all the witnesses are examined'. Other newspapers from the time appear to have followed their lead, as there are no transcripts of the trial. However, some episodes were reported including an absurd incident on the third day. [182]

Under the heading 'Supreme Court Scene', *The Australian* reported that Gilbert Eliott, who had previously been examined as a witness for the prosecution, took a seat near the attorney general. The defence counsel, Windeyer, objected and requested that Mr. Eliott should leave the court. He argued that Mr Eliott had not only been subpoenaed by the defence, but he was also the visiting magistrate at the factory and his presence might influence the testimony of some of the witnesses. Plunkett argued that Mr Eliott had already been examined, so he had a right to remain and his assistance was necessary in conducting the case. However, it had been made clear at the commencement of the proceedings that all witnesses should leave the court after giving evidence. Eventually, Mr Eliott left the court but then Mr. Dillon, Criminal Crown Solicitor, brought him back. Windeyer moved for contempt of court against Mr Eliott. Finally, the Chief Justice announced that he would commit them all for contempt of court, including Mr. Eliott and the Crown law officers, so Mr. Eliott was ordered to withdraw. [183]

The trial dragged on with a mass of evidence introduced into the court. *The Cumberland Times and Western Advertiser* labelled it 'The Unfathomable Factory Case' and reported that:

> The documentary statements alone filled a hand cart, which required six men to drag it: all of which the counsel pro. and con. seem inclined to inflict upon the luckless jury: for their own part, they are careful to avoid it as much as possible. At best this is a vile and ridiculous farce: and reminds us that the (threadbare) anagram for lawyers is "Slyware!" Were the movers of this piece of machiavellianism of any other profession, we might be induced to appeal to their conscience; but while Mr. Windeyer gets his ten guineas, and Mr.

Michie fingers his five daily, we cannot venture upon so hopeless an attempt. [184]

The trial was conducted from 9.30am and adjourned at about 4pm, 'in order to enable the Jurors and witnesses from Parramatta and its vicinity to reach their homes by the evening boat from Sydney.' To make matters drag on even further, counsel for the defence insisted that all the documents should be read aloud, probably as a delaying tactic, even though they consisted almost entirely of figures. This took four days:

> The Supreme Court for the last two days has been the scene of one of the greatest burlesques upon the administration of justice that has come under our notice ... In law every person is entitled to have the whole of any document read any part of which is given in evidence against him ... The reading commenced at the opening of the court on a Monday and was continued the whole day a second clerk being brought down to "take a spell" occasionally... The returns are all figures and the reading of them is enough to turn the brain of those compelled to listen. Only conceive the martyrdom of being forced for two entire days to listen to a clerk reading in a monotonous voice, "March 1st, 258; 2, 258; 3, 258.' ...hour after hour, the only variation being an occasional... "quantity of coals consumed". Mr Windeyer, to show that he did not consider the matter of much importance, went away altogether, the Solicitor-General amused himself by reading Moliere...some of the jurors were reading novels, other (more enlightened men) were reading yesterday's *Herald*, two or three had some illustrated

papers, while one, without the least attempt at disguise, went to sleep. [185]

On 20 October, the court adjourned until 9 December. Various witnesses for the trial were becoming increasingly frustrated as the case dragged on, and they received no compensation for their time. The attorney general requested compensation for them as, 'they complained of the hardship and inconvenience they suffer by the attendance at so tedious a trial'. But the governor said he had limited funds for contingent expenses. One of the witnesses, John Johnson, a previous clerk at the factory, complained that he had no job and would be forced to leave Sydney for the 'interior' unless he could be given a, 'temporary situation with the Government.' [186]

Members of the jury also sought compensation. The governor had already approved a payment of £15 per person for the jury in June 1845. In October, William Cox, foreman of the jury, wrote to the judges requesting some recompense for, 'the length of time it has already occupied, the expense many of the jury who reside in the country are subject to and the loss sustained by all.' The Chief Justice wrote to the governor seeking some 'consideration' for the jury, noting that, 'the jury Laws <u>are defective</u>, in having made no provision for cases, so extremely protracted as those of the two Banks' case, & the present one of Hamilton & Bell.'

Governor Gipps refused, saying that he doubted if he could, 'either increase or reduce that allowance without assuming to himself authority superior to the Law.' [187]

The court resumed on 9 December and sat until 11 December 1845. The attorney general closed the case for the Crown, even though one of the witnesses for the Crown, John Ward, was absent. Surgeon Gordon Gwynne provided a medical certificate confirming that Ward was, 'laboring under a very severe attack of delirium tremens', which is confusion usually caused by withdrawal from alcohol. The court decided that even with this absence, there was ample evidence to sustain the prosecution's case.

On 12 December, Windeyer commenced the case for the defence. After two hours, he asked the court to adjourn to the following day and, despite objection from the attorney general, the case was adjourned. The next day, William Cox, the foreman of the jury was absent and a medical certificate was tabled stating that he had an attack of gout. Once again the trial was adjourned, this time until January 1846.

The trial reconvened on 7 January and William Cox was still ill. The judges then decided to terminate the trial because, without a complete jury, they had no power to adjourn the case further. [188]

Governor Gipps was still determined that justice would not be thwarted. He instructed the attorney general to set a date for a new trial. Plunkett carried out his direction and the trial was set down for 6 April 1846. Plunkett explained that:

> The case of the Crown was fully sustained by the evidence; and it is to be regretted for the sake of Public Justice that its ends should have been delayed so long perhaps ultimately defeated by the course the trial has taken ... altho' I feel it my duty to persevere in bringing the Defendants to Justice, as far as in my power lies, I cannot be certain of procuring all the witnesses who were examined on the last trial. They are now scattered in various parts of the Colony, and I fear the attendance of some of them cannot be counted on. [189]

The attorney general was not the only one who felt that the trial had gone on too long:

> After the expense which the colony, as well as the defendants in the matter of the Queen v. Bell and Hamilton, have been ... needlessly put to, we find that Her Majesty's Attorney-General is about to commence proceedings de novo against the said defendants in the Criminal Court ... we cannot but express our surprise at that officer's ultimate determination. [190]

On 8 April 1846 the trial was finally aborted because an important witness for the Crown had left the colony. Governor Gipps accepted this result but regretted that, 'in the case both of Mr Bell and Mr Hamilton, the ends of justice will be defeated.' [191]

There were a number of reasons for the long delays in the conduct of this court case. The Supreme Court had given priority to other trials, such as *Bank of Australasia V the Bank of Australia*. Also the prosecution needed to seek documentary evidence from Britain which delayed the trial for a year. This played right into the hands of the defence. The longer the trial took, the more ways key witnesses, or members of the jury, could: succumb to one of the many deadly diseases; abscond or leave the colony; or not attend because of the severe financial toll the trial was taking on them. During the adjournments, Windeyer had warned of the consequences of delays and a drawn out trial, thinking that witnesses necessary for his defence, may disperse throughout the colony, or leave it entirely. In fact, a key witness eventually did leave the colony but it actually assisted the defence because the trial had to be aborted.

Thomas was now free. He and Sarah must have been very grateful to their legal team in achieving this result, although their legal costs must have been substantial. In official documentation, Thomas always maintained his innocence. However, the evidence presented by the defence at the committal hearing certainly does not support this view.

After the trial was aborted, Thomas sought compensation. He also applied for other jobs in government but was not successful on either count. His reputation had been severely damaged, and consequently he sought other avenues to rebuild his and his family's lives.

CHAPTER 9.

'Town clock':

from **PARRAMATTA FEMALE FACTORY**
to the **DARLING DOWNS**

The legal proceedings would have taken a huge emotional and financial toll on Thomas and his family. The Bells' sons, John and Marmaduke, may still have been living with their parents somewhere in Parramatta, and Joshua was working in a solicitor's office in Sydney. Their daughter, Mary Isabella Macdonald may also have returned to live with Thomas and Sarah as her husband, John Macdonald, had died at the end of 1845, and their house was advertised for sale in January of the next year. [192]

Sarah's life during the trial must have been very difficult as she had held a respected position as matron of the factory. Once her husband was charged, she faced shame and embarrassment and, perhaps, it took a toll on her health. She also may have needed to find other work, as years later her second son, John Alexander, advised his daughter that she may need to find work, 'as [a] Governess as my mother had to do'. [193]

During the many postponements of the court case, Thomas would have consulted with his legal team. He was also probably looking around for other opportunities, as his chances of obtaining another government job would have looked bleak. Many people were taking up land, and the Bells may have always planned to do this. However, once they obtained salaries and the opportunity for some 'material enterprise' at the factory, this plan may have been deferred.

Since the 1820s, settlers had increasingly taken up land beyond the 'limits of location' in NSW which was roughly 400 kilometres from Sydney. These settlers were called squatters and they settled illegally on the land. By 1836, their numbers had increased, so Governor Bourke introduced a system whereby they had temporary occupancy of this Crown land, for an annual licence fee of £10. Land commissioners were appointed to administer the system.

The Darling Downs, named by Alan Cunningham who was the first white explorer to reach the area in 1827, was in the north of the colony of NSW. It was gazetted in 1843, with Governor Gipps appointing Christoper Rolleston as its first Commissioner of Crown Lands. [194]

In the same year, Thomas was approached by Arthur Hodgson, a settler on the Darling Downs, to buy the stock and improvements on a tract of land on the Darling Downs called Gimba. Hodgson had been commissioned by Mr Griffiths of Griffiths and Anning (solicitors), to, 'take delivery of the stock and station [Gimba] on behalf of the trustees of Richard Scougall's estate'. Scougall had been declared bankrupt. Hodgson put Henry Dennis in charge of Gimba, and Dennis told him that his friend, Thomas Bell, may be interested in purchasing the stock and improvements.

Consequently, when Arthur Hodgson went to Sydney, he visited Thomas at Parramatta to seek his interest. The next day (the exact date of the purchase is unclear), Thomas purchased, 'all sheep, cattle, and all improvements for £3 200'. On 6 March 1844, Thomas paid the annual licence fee, of £10, for Gimba, covering the period 1 July 1843 to 30 June 1844. On 10 October 1844, he renewed the licence over this pastoral run, now known as Jimba, for another year. [195]

Was Thomas aware he was settling on Aboriginal land or did he take up land under the premise that it was nobody's land (terra nullius)?

Aboriginal people had been living on this land for thousands of years. When squatters commenced arriving in the early 1840s and settling on their land, it prevented Aboriginal people from leading their traditional ways. Consequently, they resisted this occupation which culminated in specific actions by settlers, such as the poisoning of many Aboriginal peoples at Kilcoy Station. A campaign of resistance against the settlers commenced. This campaign was unfolding at the time Thomas secured the licence on Gimba, the land inhabited by the Barungam Aboriginal language group. With thousands of sheep and cattle on Aboriginal land, Thomas must have known that he, his sons and his workers, many of whom would have been convicts or ex-convicts, could be in danger. [196]

Thomas probably spent limited time on Jimba during the next couple of years, as Henry Dennis was managing the run. It would have been an arduous trip travelling by steamer from Sydney to Moreton Bay, and then by horse or dray, from Brisbane to Ipswich. The trip from Ipswich to Jimba would have been even more onerous.

Thomas was at Jimbour when Ludwig Leichhardt left from there on his trip to Port Essington on the Coburg Peninsula, Northern Territory. Leichhardt recorded in his diary, of 1 October 1844, that:

> After having repaired some harness, which had been broken by our refractory bullocks upsetting their loads, and after my companions had completed their arrangements, in which Mr. Bell kindly assisted, we left Jimba, and launched, buoyant with hope, into the wilderness of Australia. [197]

However, Thomas was still aggrieved by his dismissal from the female factory and determined to receive compensation, for what he perceived as a great injustice. In June 1846, once the court case was aborted, he prepared a petition. He sought compensation for his removal from office, restoration to his former position and indemnity for the expenses which he incurred in the course of the proceedings against him by the government. He also sought, 'an additional allowance, for which he had been recommended to the Secretary of State for 1843.' Governor Gipps noted on this petition:

> during the early years of Mr Bell's employment at the Factory I considered him an active, a zealous, and a very useful Officer, I have every reason to believe that, in the years 1842 and 1843, he fell into bad practices; and since that time I have considered him entirely unworthy of confidence, or of any indulgence from Her Majesty's Government; indeed I cannot but be of the opinion…that in his case the ends of justice have been signally defeated. [198]

Thomas' petition was rejected. [199]

Two years later, Thomas was once again on the Darling Downs when Ludwig Leichhardt began his first attempt to reach the west coast of Australia and, ultimately, the Swan River. In January

1847, an update of Leichhardt's whereabouts reached the southern newspapers:

> We have been favoured by Mr. Bell, of Darling Downs, with the following particulars of the exploring party under Dr. Leichhardt … The party had arrived in safety at the station, of Mr. Bell, on Sunday, 6th instant … After resting on the last Sabbath day within the precincts of civilised society, the party started on their route, having had their stock augmented by a donation of twenty wethers from the flocks of Mr. Bell … Mr. Bell's son, John Alexander Bell, volunteered to accompany him… [200]

John Mann, a member of the expedition, wrote in his diary, a week later, that the expedition was at Charley's Creek. Five 'natives' were camped close by and visited them:

> One of the men introduced himself as "Mr Bell" and another as "Mr Dennis"; they had, no doubt, obtained these names from the owners of Jimbour. An old pair of trousers, which had gone the round of the tribe, and were sewn together by kangaroo sinew, was the only article of clothing possessed by the lot. [201]

Despite reestablishing himself and his family on the Darling Downs, Thomas had still not given up trying to regain his previous position. He believed Gilbert Eliott was to blame and he wanted to get his revenge. In January 1847, he saw an opportunity. The new Governor, Sir Charles Fitzroy, had dismissed Mr and Mrs Smyth, the current storekeeper and matron, who had replaced the Bells at the factory. They were being removed for poor conduct after giving a ball on the premises, 'which led to a scene of intoxication, riot and insubordination among the women.'

Thomas wrote to Deputy Commissary, General Ramsay, on 22 January 1847 saying that he had just arrived back after several months away, probably at Jimbour seeing off Leichhardt. He had discovered that the Smyths had been, 'experiencing almost similar treatment at the hands of the Visiting Justice …and, have been subjected to similar charges of embezzlement and to similar embarrassment in the performance of their duties.'

He attached a declaration from the Smyths, which stated that Gilbert Eliott's washing and needlework were being done at the factory, and that the hospital was being supplied with soap from the laundry. They claimed that this:

> was a subject of frequent conversation by Mr Eliott, who said there was a necessity of curtailing the expense of the Soap, as it was the Principal charge against Bell … as he often said, if he could not convict Bell on any other charge, they had him on the hip for the Hospital Soap.

Thomas' complaints were forwarded to the colonial secretary who sought responses from Gilbert Eliott and Dr Pat Hill. Eliott's response was that he had never spoken to the Smyths about Thomas, and his washing and needlework were done at the factory, because all staff at the factory, including the Bells, enjoyed this privilege. Dr Hill explained that the original charge against Thomas did not relate to the quantity of soap used at the hospital, but that soap drawn for the hospital had not been used by the hospital. Thomas' complaint was dismissed. [202]

Sarah Bell

But worse was to come. A month later Thomas received the terrible news that Henry Dennis, his manager at Jimbour, was one of the 44 people who died when the *Sovereign* sank in Moreton Bay on 11 March 1847. Dennis had been travelling to Sydney to marry Mary Isabella Macdonald, the Bell's widowed daughter. Thomas immediately left on 21 March 1847 aboard the *Tamar* for Moreton Bay and, a month later, Messrs. Bell (probably Joshua and John Bell) left on the same steamer, presumably to take over the management of Jimbour. [203]

Sarah remained at Parramatta and, probably, never went to Jimbour. All her children moved away with Joshua and John Bell managing Jimbour on the Darling Downs and Marmaduke moving to England to attend St Augustine's College at Canterbury. Mary Isabella had married Thomas de Lacy Moffatt on 17 April 1850, and had moved to Ipswich in Queensland. [204]

It appears that Thomas also remained in Parramatta visiting the Darling Downs, periodically. He had still not given up hope of a government job. On 21 July 1849, he wrote to the colonial secretary, offering his services for the soon to be vacant position of principal gaoler at Darlinghurst Goal. In the letter he referred to:

> my long services under the Government having first served
> as Superintendent of the Immigrant Barracks many years
> ago, subsequently at Carters Barracks, and afterwards
> for several year over the Female Factory at Parramatta …

[where Thomas had] … brought that Establishment to such a state of regularity and wholesome Discipline as has not been surpassed, if equalled, in this Colony; and but for the malicious prosecution instituted against me by ill-disposed parties the Government up to this day, might have reaped the advantages of my experience.

A terse note by Govenor Charles Fitzroy, written in the margin of Thomas' letter, makes it clear that Thomas's career in government was over. 'Mr Bell, whose career in connection with the Govt is well known to me. I should certainly not sanction his engagement under Govt in that or any other capacity.' [205]

Perhaps, the shame and despair of the court case affected Sarah Bell's health. She died after a four day illness on 12 June 1853, at only 50 years of age. Her death notice revealed nothing about her life only who her father and husband had been:

Sarah Bell's headstone: Beneath are interred the remains of Sarah Bell the beloved wife of Mr Thomas Bell of Parramatta who died June 12 1853 aged 50 years.

> Died. At Parramatta, on Sunday, June 12, after
> 4 days' illness, Sarah, wife of Mr. Thomas Bell,
> second daughter of the late John Alexander
> Esq., of Maryville Gort, County of Galway,
> Ireland, aged 50 years. [206]

It must have been a sad funeral at St John's Church as Thomas may have been the only family member there. The service was conducted by Reverend Henry Bobart, who had officiated at her daughter's wedding to Thomas de Lacy Moffat, three years before.

Sarah was buried in St John's Cemetery and Thomas would have arranged for a headstone to be erected. The Bell Family Bible records that, 'Her remains lies in Capt Moffatts Tomb in the St John's Burial Ground.' Captain Robert Gerald Moffatt, a magistrate at Parramatta from 1834 till 1843, had probably bought a burial plot in St John's Cemetery while living at Parramatta and had then moved to the Darling Downs. He may have known the Bells while living at Parramatta, and the association became closer when the Bells' daughter married his nephew, Thomas de Lacy Moffatt. When Captain Moffatt died on the Darling Downs on 17 March 1848 and was buried there, the plot in St John's Cemetery became vacant. Thomas de Lacy Moffatt, now Sarah's son-in-law, probably suggested that Sarah be buried in his uncle's tomb. [207]

With no government position and his wife Sarah deceased, Thomas Bell decided to move to Queensland. In August 1853, two months after Sarah died, he placed an advertisement in *The Sydney Morning Herald*. He described himself as, 'a Gentleman about to travel into the interior', who wished to purchase a daguerreotype camera, plates and cases with the equipment suitable for views and portraits. He stated that he needed the camera on or before 1 September 1853, and it could be delivered to Russell's Hotel at

123 Pitt Street. Thomas may have been staying there before moving to the Darling Downs or provided this address, because the hotel's long room also operated as an auction venue. [208]

Thomas spent the rest of his life at Ipswich and on Jimbour station. His sons, Joshua and John, took over the daily management of Jimbour under the company name of Bell and Sons. Thomas may not have taken an active part in the work on Jimbour, and probably spent a good deal of time in Ipswich. He bought a substantial amount of land over the years in Ipswich, including over 100 acres of land in 1860 and, in July 1861, 14 acres at £5 per acre, near the racecourse at Ipswich. [209]

Thomas Bell, 1864

He eventually built and owned a house at Waterstown and, in March 1872, a deposit of coal was found on this property. His daughter's (Mary Isabella) family, the de Lacy Moffatts, lived with him at Waterston. She died in Paris in 1866, only two years after the death of her husband Thomas de Lacy Moffatt. After her death, John Alexander Bell and his family lived with Thomas until his death on 5 September 1872, aged 74 after a short illness. Two months after his death, John Alexander, his family and the de Lacy Moffatt children left for England. [210]

Thomas' obituary in the *Ipswich and General Advertiser* shows that, in his almost 20 years in Ipswich and on the Darling Downs, he had reinvented himself as a respected and philanthropic citizen:

> He was noted for his benevolence and liberality; he
> always took a very prominent part in every matter

of charity, and was one of the prime movers in the foundation of Ipswich Hospital. Mr Bell's horse and buggy, which appeared in town every morning at an early business hour, with such regularity as to have been commonly termed the "town clock" will now be missed by many who were in the habit of looking out for it almost as much as the mail. [211]

On the day of his burial the procession stopped at St Paul's Church where the first part of the burial service was conducted and the organ, donated by Thomas and his son-in-law, Thomas de Lacy Moffatt, played, 'a mournful strain as the body entered the church.' The procession then travelled to the Ipswich Cemetery and he was buried in the Moffatt and Bell families grave. [212]

Moffat and Bell family grave, Ipswich General Cemetery. The white marble memorial has the words 'This memorial is erected in loving memory of their father by the sons of Thomas Bell who died Waterston, Ipswich September 5, 1872 aged 74 years.'

Conclusion

Thomas and Sarah Bell had gambled on making the treacherous journey from Ireland to NSW, in the hope that they could provide a better life for themselves and their family. They may have intended to establish themselves on land, but discovered, on arriving in NSW, that free grants of land had ceased at the beginning of 1831. Land in the 'settled areas' could only be bought by auction. Consequently, with little or no capital, Thomas Bell proceeded to take jobs in the civil service.

Life would have been very different for the Bells if Thomas had been convicted of the offences, with which he was charged. It appears he was only saved from this outcome through the work of a good lawyer, and the continuous delays and final abandonment of the case.

As news of the court case appeared regularly in the daily press, Thomas may have been looking for opportunities to remove his family from Sydney and had probably heard about the fortunes that settlers could make on large tracts of land in the interior. He seized the opportunity to establish his family on the Darling Downs when he took out a licence, and purchased the stock and improvements on Jimbour. However it was a risky strategy, to be spending this large amount of money, when he was being accused of defrauding the government. There is no transcription of his trial, so it is unclear whether this purchase was ever raised in the evidence, or if it was public knowledge.

Thomas lived for another 22 years during which time his family prospered on the Darling Downs. Sadly, the Bells' daughter, Mary Isabella de Lacy Moffatt, died at the young age of 41 and the eldest son, Joshua, died in 1881, at only 54 years of age. The Bells, through a combination of bad management, droughts and the depression of the 1890s, eventually lost Jimbour Station after having been associated with the property for almost 50 years.

Acknowledgements

Writing the story of my great-great-grandparents has been a much bigger job than I ever imagined, and I would not have completed it without the support of a number of people.

I would like to thank my sister, Diana Bell, who found the original references to the Bells as matron and keeper at the Parramatta Female Factory and spent time with me at the NSW State Archives tracking down references to our relatives. I would also like to thank my husband, Ron Micola, who has provided me with moral support and encouragement throughout the process. He even accompanied me to the NSW State Archives to help me with further research for this book, and read and reread many iterations of the various chapters. My sons, Timothy and Simon, have always been very encouraging and read various drafts and provided me with very useful suggestions.

I am also grateful to historian, Jennifer Harrison, who has encouraged me from the beginning and also read a very early draft of the book and provided valuable feedback. Also thanks to Janice Cooper, from the Genealogical Society of Queensland, Anne Mathews, from the Parramatta Female Factory Friends and Anne Robotham for reading drafts and providing comments.

Thanks also to Todd Doyle for all his help in preparing this book for publication and his very effective cover design.

Notes

Abbreviations used in the endnotes

ADB   Australian Dictionary of Biography

AJCP   Australian Joint Copying Project

CO   Colonial Office

HRA   Historical Records of Australia

NSWSA   New South Wales State Archives

NRS   New South Wales Records Series

Instead of manually typing the (often lengthy) links in
the notes, we recommend visiting the companion website:
academyforyoungladies.com

1   https://modhistorymusings.com/2019/09/13/writing-the-biography-of-sarah-bell-for-the-st-johns-cemetery-project/   accessed 10 August 2021.

2   The places of their births come from the certificates of birth for Sarah and Thomas's grandchildren in the Queensland, Births, Deaths and Marriages and the Certificate of Death, Thomas Bell, No. 361, 5 September 1872. Place of birth for the Bells' son Marmaduke is listed in the following link which may not be accurate. http://collection.hht.net.au/firsthht/fullRecordPicture.jsp?recnoListAttr=recnoListRI&recno=53678 accessed 10 August 2021.

3   A Salt, *Those Outcast Women: The Female Factory 1821–1848*, Hale & Iremonger, Sydney, 1984; G Hendrikson, *Conviction: The 1827 Fight for Rights at the Parramatta Female Factory*, Rowan Tree Published Books, n.d.; The Parramatta Heritage Centre, *Women Transported: Life in Australia's Convict Female Factories*, Parramatta, 2008; L Heath (MA Thesis), The Female Factories of New South Wales and Van Diemen's Land: an Examination of their role in Control, Punishment and Reformation of Prisoners between 1804 and 1854. Canberra, ANU.

4   HRA, Ser. 1, Vol. 18, p. 534, and HRA, Ser. 1 Vol. 22, p. 743.

5   J Phillips, *Old Ipswich Days: Joshua Peter Bell and the Ipswich Connection*, Ipswich, Joyce Phillips, 2008. Bell, Sir Joshua Peter (1827-1881), ADB http://adb.anu.edu.au/biography/bell-sir-joshua-peter-2969 accessed 10 August 2021.

6   'Proposed Society of Artist', *The Sydney Morning Herald*, 27 March, 1850, p.13, col. 2. http://nla.gov.au/nla.news-article12916701; 'The Fine Arts', *The Maitland Mercury and Hunter River General Advertiser*, 11 December, 1850, p. 4. col. 3-4.

http://nla.gov.au/nla.news-article687590; 'Death', *The Maitland Mercury and Hunter River General Advertiser*, 30 April, 1851, p. 3. col. 3. http://nla.gov.au/nla.news-article684234   accessed 10 August 2021. D Philips, *William Augustus Miles (1796-1851): crime, policing and moral entrepreneurship in England and Australia*, Melbourne, History Department, University of Melbourne (University of Melbourne history monographs: no. 30), 2001, pp. 182-88.

7   NSWSA: NRS 905, [4/2574.1] 42/4529 Enclosed 42/837, William Augustus Miles to Colonial Secretary, 29 January 1842;   [4/2610.1] 43/1488 Enclosed 43/1347, Memorandum from Governor Gipps, 20 February 1843.

8   'Domestic Intelligence Drayton', *The Moreton Bay Courier*, 1 October 1853, p. 2, col. 3-4. http://nla.gov.au/nla.news-article3711530 'Bell V Pearce', *The Moreton Bay Courier*, 20 May 1854, pp 2-3, col. 7.

9   E Rushen & P McIntyre, *Fair Game: Australia's first immigrant women*, Sydney, Anchor Books, 2010, pp. 12-14. The five commissioners included Lord Howick, Under-Secretary for the Colonies. S McConville, *Irish Political Prisoners, 1848-1922*, London, Routledge, 2003, p. 89, note 174. Samuel Lapham from Athy, County Kildare. Police magistrate and Superintendent of Convicts, Maria Island & dismissed because too lenient.

10   *Lloyd's Register of British and Foreign Shipping*, 1831, London, Society for the Registry of Shipping. https://books.google.co.uk/books?id=MzkSAAAAYAAJ

11   NSWSA: NRS 905, [4/2610.1] 43/6173, Enclosing 38/13188, Memo No.2 Memorial by Thomas Bell, n.d. but about December 1838.   Chelsea pensioner, a retired soldier who had lived as a pensioner at the Royal Hospital, Chelsea or Royal Hospital Kilmainham, Dublin or on a military pension elsewhere. By 1820s there was a large increase in pensioners so this scheme was an attempt to reduce costs.

12   Backhouse, *A Narrative of a Visit to the Australian Colonies*, London, Hamilton, Adams, and Co, 1843, pp. 1-2.

13   A Bourke, 'Journal of a Voyage to Australia', SLN, pp. 35-36.

14   A Bourke, 'Journal of a Voyage to Australia', pp.11 and 20.

15   Bell Family Bible held by Anita O'Connor, Sligo, County Galway, Ireland.

16   'The Courier', *The Hobart Town Courier*, 5 May 1832, p. 2, col. 2. http://nla.gov.au/nla.news-article4199509 'Shipping Intelligence', *The Sydney Gazette and NSW Advertiser*, 12 May 1832, p. 2 col.1. http://nla.gov.au/nla.news-article2206538 accessed 10 August 2021. J Backhouse, *A Narrative of a Visit to the Australian Colonies*, p. 232.

17   'Accidents, Offences, &c', *The Sydney Herald*, 14 February 1833, p. 3, col. 4. http://nla.gov.au/nla.news-article28654190 accessed 10 August 2021.

18   WA Miles, 'Sketches of Europe and Australia', ca. 1834-50'. PXA537, SLN. https://convictrecords.com.au/ships/burrell/1831 (arrival of Burrell) accessed 10 August 2021.

19   NSWSA: NRS 905, [4/2610.1] 43/6173, Enclosing 38/13188, Memo No.2, Memorial by Thomas Bell, 28 May 1838. Governor's Correspondence, 1832 to 1844, File 114, AJCP Role 1046, (From Records of the Colonial Office, Index of Incoming

Correspondence, (CO 714), NSW. https://nla.gov.au/nla.obj-1208748209/view
Viscount Howick was Henry George Grey, Under-Secretary for Colonies 1830-33.
Shipping list for Thomas Bell on *Cleopatra* lists him as Esquire. 'The Public Money',
The Australian 23 March 1832, p.2. col.3. http://nla.gov.au/nla.news-article42009608
accessed 10 August 2021.

20   HRA, Ser. 1, Vol. 17, 8 May 1835, p.725. The building was demolished in early 1834
after *Layton* arrived and the women were housed in temporary buildings behind
Government House. The other ship used in the trial was *Princess Royal* which went
to Hobart Town.

21   'The Free Females by the Red Rover', *The Sydney Monitor*, 15 August 1832, p.2,
col.1, http://nla.gov.au/nla.news-article32141886 accessed 10 August 2021.
E. Rushen and P McIntyre, *Fair Game.*

22   'Female Emigration', *The Sydney Gazette and New South Wales Advertiser*, 3 February
1835, p. 2. col. 5. Extract of a letter from an unnamed female emigrant.
http://nla.gov.au/nla.news-article2197232 accessed 10 August 2021.

23   NSWSA: NRS 905, [4/2152] 32/7205, 32/5943, 32/7079, Thomas Bell to Colonial
Secretary 18, 21, 25 and 26 Sept 1832. [4/2152] 32/7359 & 32/7503, Colonial
Treasurer to Colonial Secretary, 2 and 9 October 1832. [4/2152] 32/5943, Report
to Governor Bourke, 9 January 1833. E. Rushen and P McIntyre, *Fair Game*, pp.
72-76.

24   NSWSA: Colonial Secretary; Returns of the Colony (Blue Books), 1832, Microfiche 2. NSWSA, NRS 905, [4/2317.2] 36/7407 Enclosed 36/7214], W. Lithgow
to Colonial Secretary, 6 September 1836; 4/2247, [33/448], Petition from James
Sparkes, August 1833. E. Rushen and P McIntyre, *Fair Game*, pp. 69-70.

25   'Domestic Intelligence', The Sydney Herald, 4 July 1833, p. 3. col. 5.
http://nla.gov.au/nla.news-article12847195 accessed 10 August 2021.

26   NSWSA, Colonial Secretary, Returns of the Colony (Blue Books), Microfiche,
1833, 1834, 1835. Thomas Bell's role superintending the migrant women is not
listed although 1835 Blue Book reveals he received 5s per diem as Superintendent
of Emigrants. HRA, Ser. 1, Vol. 17, 13 February 1835, p. 661. E. Rushen and P
McIntyre, *The Merchant's Women*, Anchor Books, 2008, p. 48.

27   NSWSA: NRS 905, [4/2273.3] 35/2962, Thomas Bell to Colonial Secretary, 21
April 1835. *The Sydney Gazette and NSW Advertiser*, 14 March 1835, p.2. col. 6.
http://nla.gov.au/nla.news-article2197562 accessed 10 August 2021. Elizabeth
Rushen, *Single & Free: female migration to Australia, 1833-1837*, Anchor Books
Australia, Sydney, pp.104-105.

28   *The Sydney Gazette and New South Wales Advertiser*, 22 December 1835, p. 2. col. 7.
http://nla.gov.au/nla.news-article2201822 accessed 10 August 2021. NSWSA,
Colonial Secretary, *Returns of the Colony* (Blue Books), Microfiche, 1836.

29   HRA, Ser. I, Vol. 10, 27 July 1822, p. 686. 'The Debtors', *The Sydney Gazette and
New South Wales Advertiser*, 3 December 1835, p. 3, col. 4. https://trove.nla.gov.au/
newspaper/article/2201512 accessed 10 August 2021. J Bryson, 'Debtors' prison and
the rules of the prison'. *Bar News: The Journal of the NSW Bar Association*, Summer
2019, Dec 2019, pp 58-61.

30 'Corpe v Bell and another', *The Sydney Monitor*, 29 June 1836, p.3. col. 1.
    http://www.austlii.edu.au/au/other/NSWSupC/1836/47.html
    accessed 9 March 2023.

31 Email from Christine Fernon, Online Centre, National Centre of Biography,
    24 February 2020. https://www.sydgram.nsw.edu.au/community/school-archives/
    The register of Sydney College lists the Bell children's addresses as Carters' Barracks.
    accessed 10 August 2021.

32 'Piano Forte Instruction', *The Sydney Herald*, 9 September 1833, p. 2. col. 5. http://
    nla.gov.au/nla.news-article12847682 'For Sale', *The Sydney Herald*, 18 December
    1837, p. 1. col. 6. http://nla.gov.au/nla.news-article12862950 accessed 10 August
    2021.

33 'Principal Superintendent of Convicts' Office, Sydney, 19th August, 1834', *New
    South Wales Government Gazette*, 20 August 1834, p. 600, col. 2. http://nla.gov.au/
    nla.news-article230687265   ' Police Office', *The Sydney Monitor*, 8 October 1834,
    p. 3. col. 2. http://nla.gov.au/nla.news-article32147331 This report says Selina came
    on the *Sovereign* but she came on the *Southworth*. 'Police Incidents', *The Australian*,
    7 October 1834, p.2. col.5. http://nla.gov.au/nla.news-article42009511 accessed 10
    August 2021. convictrecords.com.au Recorded as Selina McGary and McGarry.

34 'Police Office', *The Sydney Monitor*, 28 November 1835, p. 2-3. col. 6. http://nla.gov.
    au/nla.news-article32150217 convictrecords.com.au   Ann Putter was sentenced to
    14 years at Surry Quarter Sessions and transported on *George Hibbert* arriving on 1
    December 1834. accessed 10 August 2021.

35 D Oxley, *Convict Maids: the Forced Migration of Women to Australia.* Melbourne,
    Cambridge University Press, 1996. pp 43, 51, 55.

36 Salt, A, *These Outcast Women*, p. 70. Governor Brisbane made additional changes to
    factory so each class had own kitchen, workshops and accommodation. The Second
    Female Factory: 1818-1848, Geoff Barker, Parramatta Heritage Centre, 2015
    https://historyandheritage.cityofparramatta.nsw.gov.au/blog/2015/07/28/
    the-second-parramatta-female-factory-1818-1848   accessed 10 August 2021.

37 Salt, A, *These Outcast Women*, pp, 72-75.

38 NSWSA: NRS 905, [4/2317.2] 36/6164, 4 August 1836. Annotation on Ann
    Gordon by Governor Bourke on Minutes of Proceedings of Factory Committee.

39 HRA, Ser. 1, Vol. 18, 10 September 1836, p. 533.

40 H Golder, *Politics, Patronage and Public Works: the Administration of New South Wales,
    Volume 1, 1842-1900.* UNSW Press, 2005, p. 85.

41 HRA, Ser. 1, Vol. 18, 10 September 1836, p. 533-34.

42 HRA, Ser. 1, Vol. 19, 7 November 1837, pp.156-58. A Salt, *Those Outcast Women*,
    p. 60. CO, Series 201, NSW, Original Correspondence, 1783-1900. Miscellaneous
    Individuals, A-F, 1838, File 281, AJCP Reel No: 315-316, 'Parramatta Female
    Factory 1838: Correspondence between Secretary of State for Colonial Depart-
    ment and the Governors of the Australian Provinces on the Subject of Secondary
    Punishment', pp, 5-6.

43 NSWSA: NRS 905, Microfiche, 4/3722, No 36, 176 p.332. Macleay to Committee,
    11 Aug 1836.

44 J Backhouse, *A Narrative of a Visit to the Australian Colonies*, p. 238.

45 NSWSA: NRS 909, Governor's Minutes and Memoranda, 4/999, M3694, 21 August 1836.   Email from Jenny Pearce, The Kings School, 21 February 2020. Joshua is listed as attending Kings from 1836-42.

46 NSWSA: NRS 909, Governor's Minutes and Memoranda, 4/999, M3694, 21 August 1836. HRA, Ser. 1, Vol. 18, p. 534. *New South Wales Government Gazette*, 7 September 1836, p. 705. Number of women and children in the Female Factory. http://nla.gov.au/nla.news-article230673064

47 'News of the Day,' *The Sydney Monitor*, 10 October 1836, p.2, col. 3. http://nla.gov.au/nla.news-article32152424 accessed 10 August 2021.

48 A Salt, *These Outcast Women*, pp.117-18.

49 J Backhouse, *A Narrative of a Visit to the Australian Colonies*, p. 301.

50 'Various documents collected by Sir William Dixson, Item 3 Rules for the Government of the Female Factory, Matron', 28 February 1839.

51 'The Female Factory', *The Australian*, 6 September, 1836, p. 2. col. 3. http://nla.gov.au/nla.news-article36853583 accessed 10 August 2021.

52 NSWSA: NRS 905, [4/2359.1] 37/2667 and 37/2773. Wme Macpherson to Colonial Secretary, 15 March 1837 and Thomas Bell to Colonial Secretary, 20 March 1837. 'Police', *The Sydney Monitor*, 23 January 1837, p. 2. col. 4. http://nla.gov.au/nla.news-article32154645 'Convict Records: Ellen Pollard', https://convictrecords.com.au/convicts/pollard/ellen/103920 accessed 10 August 2021.

53 NSWSA: NRS 905, [4/2359.1] 37/9598, Enclosing 37/9460, Thomas Bell to Colonial Secretary, 14 October 1836, Frederic Ebhart to Governor Bourke, 9 October 1837, Patrick McCallaghan to Governor Bourke, n.d.

54 NSWSA: NRS 905, [4/2359.1] 37/4262 Enclosing 37/3753, Philip Dwyer to Colonial Secretary, 20 April 1837. Thomas Bell to the Colonial Secretary, 4 May 1837.

55   NSWSA: NRS 905, [4/2317.2] 36/9203 enclosing 36/8977, Thomas Bell to Colonial Secretary, 10 November 1836, Police Magistrate to Colonial Secretary, 2 November 1836. [4/2317.2] 36/10.163 enclosing 36/9709, Thomas Bell to Colonial Secretary, 5 December 1836, Police Magistrate to Colonial Secretary, 25 November 1836. Bridget Sheedey: https://www.freesettlerorfelon.com/convict_ship_hooghley_1831.htm. accessed 10 August 2021.

56 NSWSA: NRS 905, [4/2317.2] 36/8991 and 36/8705. Thomas Bell to Colonial Secretary, 3 November 1836, enclosing Thomas Bell to Sol Levein, 27 October 1836, Sol Levein to Colonial Secretary 28 October 1836. 'Convict Records: Eliza Thompson', https://convictrecords.com.au/convicts/thompson/eliza/110258 accessed 10 August 2021.

57 T Smith, 'Cumberland Hospital - the early years', *Parramatta Female Factory Friends Newsletter*, Issue no 11, October - November 2016, p.4. A Salt, *These Outcast Women*, pp. 11-16, Appendix 2.

58 NSWSA: NRS 905, [4/2317.2] 35/8670, 36/10.238, Female Factory Committee to Colonial Secretary, 23 October 1835; Pieter Campbell to Bourke, 30 November

and 6 December 1836, Thomas Bell to Pieter Campbell, 5 and 10 December 1836.
'Notice', *The Sydney Herald*, 6 June 1833, p.1. col. 1.
http://nla.gov.au/nla.news-article12846958 http://www.convictrecords.com.au
 Mary Mumford arrived *Harmony* 27 September 1827 assigned Rev Wilton,
Parramatta.' The 'Parramatta Female Factory and Midwives - a brief Introduction',
https://historyandheritage.cityofparramatta.nsw.gov.au/blog/2020/05/04/the-
parramatta-female-factory-and-midwives-a-brief-introduction
accessed 10 August 2021.

59   Protestant Female Orphan School on the Parramatta River opened in 1818 and
     Boys Orphan School was located in Sydney and then Liverpool from 1824. Catholic
     Orphan School established at Waverley in 1837 and then moved next to Female
     Factory in 1841.NSWSA: NRS 905, [4/2359.1] 37/8490 and 37/6083, Thomas Bell
     to Colonial Secretary, 1 July and 9 September 1837, Thomas Bell to Richard Sadleir,
     25 August 1837.

60   NSWSA: NRS 905, [4/2317.2] 36/7400, 36/9309, Thomas Bell to the Colonial
     Secretary, 14 September and 12 November 1836.

61   NSWSA: NRS 905, [4/2317.2], 36/8709, Thomas Bell to Colonial Secretary, 26
     October 1836. *Elizabeth* docked on 12 October 1836.

62   'Police Tuesday October, 27th', *The Sydney Monitor*, 28 October 1836, p.3. col.
     1. http://nla.gov.au/nla.news-article32152597 'Convict Records: Maria Gibson',
     http://www.convictrecords.com.au/convicts/gibson/maria/36581. accessed 10 Au-
     gust 2021.

63   NSWSA: NRS 905, [4/2317.2], 37/750, Pieter Campbell to Colonial Secretary, 31
     December 1836.

64   HRA, Ser. 1, Vol. 18, 10 September 1836, p. 534, Enclosure 2.   HRA, See. 1, Vol.
     18, pp. 611-13, 10 December 1836, Lord Glenelg's despatch did not arrive in NSW
     until 8 May 1837.

65   HRA, Ser. 1, Vol. 18, 4 May 1837, pp.747-48.

66   HRA, Ser. 1, Vol. 19, 5 July 1837, pp. 6-7; 7 November 1837, p.157.

67   NSWSA: NRS 905, [4/2610.1] 43/6173 Enclosed 38/13188, Colonial Secretary to
     Thomas Bell, 22 November 1837.

68   HRA, Ser. 1, Vol. 19, 7 Nov 1837, p.156-58.

69   NSWSA: NRS 905, [4/2610.1] 43/6173 Enclosed 38/13188, George Gray to
     Thomas Bell, 28 May 1838, Lord Glenelg to Gipps, 22 May 1838. Thomas sent
     memorial to Lord Glenelg who sought advice from Governor Gipps. The Bells
     reinstated in August 1838 and memorial dropped.

70   'The Female Factory', *The Sydney Gazette and New South Wales Advertiser*, 30 January
     1838, p.2. col. 2. http://nla.gov.au/nla.news-article2550108 Accessed 10 August
     2021.

71   NSWSA: Colonial Secretary; *Returns of the Colony* (Blue Books), 1838, Fiche 1
     4/270. 'The Emigrants, residents in the Government Domain', *The Sydney Monitor*,
     26 February 1838, p.2, col. 6. http://nla.gov.au/nla.news-article32159173
     'The Emigrants', *The Sydney Monitor*, 12 March 1838, p.2, col. 5.
     http://nla.gov.au/nla.news-article32159345 accessed 10 August 2021.

72 'Tuition', *The Sydney Herald*, 11 June 1838, p.3, col, 4. http://nla.gov.au/nla.news-article12862308 accessed 10 August 2021.

73 The Female Factory', *The Sydney Gazette and New South Wales Advertiser*, 18 August 1838, p.2. col. 5. http://nla.gov.au/nla.news-article2548701, accessed 6 August 2021.

74 HRA, Ser. 1 Vol. 19, 5 July 1837, pp. 6-7. Julia Leach's late husband had, been instructor of convicts on Norfolk Island and when died she erected handsome tomb.

75 'Arrivals', *The Colonist*, 24 January 1838, p.2. col. 1. http://nla.gov.au/nla.news-article31720343, accessed 6 August 2021.

76 CO Series 201. NSW, Original Correspondence, 1783-1900. Miscellaneous Individuals, A-F, 1838, File 281, AJCP Reel No: 315-316,'Parramatta Female Factory 1838, pp. 4-5, 9.

77 NSWSA: NRS 905, [4/2401] 38/1796, Mrs Leach to Colonial Secretary, February 19, 1838.

78 NSWSA: NRS 905, [4/2401] 38/1796, Pieter Campbell to Colonial Secretary, 19 February 1838. 'Parramatta Female Factory 1838: Correspondence between Secretary of State for Colonial Department and the Governors of the Australian Provinces', p.8.

79 HRA, Ser. 1 Vol .19, Governor Gipps to Lord Glenelg, 13 March 1838, pp. 319-21.

80 'Domestic Intelligence', *The Sydney Herald*, 19 April 1838, p. 2, col. 4. http://nla.gov.au/nla.news-article12858160 accessed 10 August 2021.

81 'Parramatta Female Factory 1838: Correspondence between Secretary of State for Colonial Department and the Governors of the Australian Provinces', p. 7.

82 'Parramatta Female Factory 1838: Correspondence between Secretary of State for Colonial Department and the Governors of the Australian Provincesy Punishment', p.7. NSWSA: NRS 905, [4/2401] 38/4586, 38/5051, Pieter Campbell to Colonial Secretary, 9 May 1838, John Clapham to Governor Gipps, 12 May 1838.

83 NSWSA: NRS 905, [4/2401.1] 38/4586, 38/ 5051, 38/4860, Pieter Campbell to Colonial Secretary, 9 May 1838, John Clapham to Governor Gipps, 12 May 1838, Thomas Bell to Colonial Secretary, 15 May 1838.

84 NSWSA: NRS 905, [4/2401.1] 38/5291, Pieter Campbell to Colonial Secretary, 26 May, 1838. Mary Mumford resigned on 21 August 1838 and Elizabeth Scott replaced her.

85 NSWSA: NRS 905, [4/2610.1] 43/6173 Enclosing 38/13188, Memo No.2 Memorial by Thomas Bell, 28 May 1838.

86 HRA, Ser. 1, Vol. 19, 7 July 1838, pp. 471. Mr and Mrs Ralph Mood', http://collection.hht.net.au/firsthhtpictures/fullRecordPicture.jsp?recnoListAttr=recnoList&recno=42056 Julia Leach married Ralph Mood at Parramatta in January 1839. She lived to 92, dying at her home in Church Street, Parramatta in August 1886. accessed 10 August 2021.

87 'Immigration', *The Colonist*, 22 August 1838, p.3. col. 2. http://nla.gov.au/nla.news-page4246103, accessed 6 August 2021.

88 'The Female Factory', *The Sydney Gazette and New South Wales Advertiser*, 18 August 1838, p.2. col. 5. http://nla.gov.au/nla.news-article2548701, accessed 10 August 2021.

89 HRA, Ser. 1 Vol. 19, 19 September 1838, p.589. NSWSA: NRS 905, [4/2451.3] 39/5938, Sarah Bell to Colonial Secretary, 22 May 1839. Note by Governor Gipps, 31 May 1839. Subordinate appointments included turnkeys, midwife, laundresses, overseer of needle room.

90 P Yeend, *King's School Register, 1831-1990*, Parramatta, Kings School, 1990, p. 38. The King's School opened at Parramatta in February 1832. Joshua and John may not have attended during 1843, or withdrawn before end of year, as not in 1843 register. L Waddy, *The King's School, 1831-1981: An account,* Parramatta, The Council of The King's School, 1981, pp. 23, 46.

91 HRA, Ser. 1, Vol. 19, 1 October 1840, p. 6.

92 Sisters of Charity of Australia Congregational Archives, SER/752/1, *The Annals of the Irish Sisters of Charity in Australia 1838-1882*, Irish Sisters of Charity, p, 71. 'State of the Female Factory, Parramatta, on Saturday, 19th January, 1839', *New South Wales Government Gazette*, 23 January 1839, p. 113, col. 1.. http://nla.gov.au/nla.news-article230382641, accessed 610 August 2021. There were 728 women and 176 children in the Female Factory.

93 *The Annals of the Irish Sisters of Charity in Australia 1838-1882,* Bishop Polding to cousin, p.44.

94 NSWSA, Colonial Secretary, NRS906, Returns of the Department of Female Factory Parramatta, *1836-1843*. 4/7327, Reel 702. A school master, or mistress was included in changes made by Governor Bourke in 1836. Agnes Clapham was school mistress from 10 February to 30 April 1838 and position not included for 1839.   SRNSW, NRS 905, [4/2492.1] 40/10034, Sarah Bell to Colonial Secretary, 8 October 1840. Sarah Bell sought gratuity for Jane Edge, school mistress, at 8d per diem which was granted and she was there until September 1843.

95 'Parramatta Female Factory 1838: Correspondence between Secretary of State for Colonial Department and the Governors of the Australian Provinces', ML Ref. A1813, pp. 5, 7.

96 NSWSA: NRS 905, [4/2401.1] 38/5281, Julia Leach to Colonial Secretary, 26 May 1838.

97 'Philanthropos letter to the *Sydney Herald*' by Dr Ullathorne in W Burton, *The State of Religion and Education in New South Wales*, London, J Cross, 1840, Appendix, no. 16. https://nla.gov.au/nla.obj-52772993/view?partId=nla.obj-88426530, accessed 10 August 2021.

98 Sisters of Charity of Australia Congregational Archives, SER/752/1, *The Annals of the Irish Sisters of Charity in Australia 1838-1882*, p. 74.

99 NSWSA, NRS 905, [4/2451.3] 39/1152, 39/1562, 39/3968 Enclosing 39/2989, List of male and female children to be sent to Male and Female Orphan Schools, S Bell, Matron, 28 January and 2 February 1839; Charles Forbes to Colonial Secretary, 6 February 1839; William Ullathorne to Colonial Secretary, 8 March 1839. Pieter Campbell left position of Visiting Magistrate on 1 March 1839 to become Acting Colonial Treasurer, 8 May 1841 returned to Britain so position became permanent.

100 HRA Ser. 1 Vol. 19, 19 September 1837, p.92. 14 October 1837, p.118.

101 T Callaghan, *The Acts and Ordinances of The Governor & Council of New South Wales and Acts of Parliament Enacted for, and applied to, the Colony, Vol. 1. Victoria 3, No. 22*, pp 532-36. Sydney, 1844. 'State of the Female Factory, Parramatta,' *New South Wales Government Gazette,* 18 September 1839, p. 1,038, col.2.; 2 October 1839, p. 1,100, col. 2; 11 December 1839, p. 1,419, col. 1. http://nla.gov.au/nla.news-article230384556 http://nla.gov.au/nla.news-article230384632 http://nla.gov.au/nla.news-article230385310, accessed 10 August 2021.

102 HRA. Ser. 1, Vol. 20, 10 February 1840, p. 499. NSWSA: Colonial Secretary; NRS 905, 4/2492.1, 40/5207, William Gray to Colonial Secretary, 15 May 1840 and Memo from Governor Gipps, 8 July 1840.

103 HRA, Ser. 1, Vol. 21, 1 October 1840, pp 1-6. William Crawford and Whitworth Russell were appointed prison inspectors in 1835 and had great influence over English prisons.

104 HRA, Ser. 1, Vol 20, 31 August 1840, p 783-4, Sub-enclosure Inspectors of Prisons to Mr S M Phillips, pp. 384-85. *An Act to abolish the transportation of Female Convicts and to provide for the more effectual punishment of female offenders, within the Colony of New South Wales, 19 November 1839, Australian Legal Information Institute (AUSTLII).* http://www.austlii.edu.au/au/legis/nsw/num_act/foa1841n3167.pdf accessed 10 August 2021.

105 HRA, Ser. 1, Vol 21, 10 October 1841, p. 539.

106 S. McCulloch, 'Gipps, Sir George (1791–1847)', ADB, National Centre of Biography, Australian National University,1966. http://adb.anu.edu.au/biography/gipps-sir-george-2098, accessed 10 August 2021.

107 HRA, Ser. 1, Vol. 21, 1 October 1840, pp. 2-4. 'State of the Female Factory, Parramatta, on Saturday 25the August 1838', *New South Wales Government Gazette,* 29 August 1838, p. 684, col. 1; 18 March 1840, p. 261, col.1. http://nla.gov.au/nla.news-article230387107 http://nla.gov.au/nla.news-article230136979, Female Factory earned £133 making articles for orphan schools and £700 from needlework done for private individuals from 1 March 1839 to 31 July 1840.

108 'The Female Factory', *The Colonist* , 26 December 1838, p.2, col. 5. http://nla.gov.au/nla.news-article31722266   accessed 10 August 2021.

109 'State of the' Female Factory, Parramatta', *New South Wales Government Gazette,* 21 August and 18 September 1839, p. 938 and p.1038. http://nla.gov.au/nla.news-article230384330 http://nla.gov.au/nla.news-article230384556, accessed 10 August 2021. HRA, Ser. 1, Vol 21, 1 October 1840, pp. 5-6.

110 NSWSA: NRS 905, [4/2492.1] 40/5541, [4/2574.1], 42/167, Sarah Bell to Colonial Secretary, 30 May 1840. Sarah Bell to Colonial Secretary, 17 January 1842. Sarah Bell's letter sent an account of ten shillings to for trousers which had been lost. Governor Gipps ordered that they be '…charged against the money earned by the women in the room out of which it was stolen.'

111 HRA, Ser. 1, Vol 21, 1 October 1840, pp. 5-6.

112 HRA, Ser. 1 Vol. 21, 1 October 1840, p. 3. Convict Ships to Australia in jenwilletts.com   accessed 8 April 2020.

113 'State of the Female Factory, Parramatta, on Saturday, 25 August, 1838', *New South Wales Government Gazette*, 29 August 1838, p. 684, col. 1. http://nla.gov.au/nla. news-article230387107, accessed 10 August 2021. NSWSA: NRS 905, [4/2451.3] 39/6389 Enclosing 39/5639, 39/6874, 39/6298, 39/6041, Charles Forbes to Colonial Secretary, 10 June 1839; Thomas Tubman to Colonial Secretary, 28 May 1839; Sarah Bell to Colonial Secretary, 27 May 1839. Some of the women were returned to their husbands.   Harrison, J, *Shackled: Female Convicts at Moreton Bay 1826-1839*, Melbourne, Anchor Books, 2016, pp.37-38, 184. 19 women were released into the community after careful checking of records.

114 NSWSA: NRS 905, [4/2401] 38/9545, 38/9756, 38/10.235, Sarah Bell to Colonial Secretary, 11 and 17 September 1838. Visiting Magistrate to Colonial Secretary, 27 September 1838.

115 NSWSA: NRS 905, [4/2451.3] 39/3666, 39/3666 Enclosed 39/2680, 39/6874, Charles Forbes to Colonial Secretary, 29 March, 1839, William Snell to Governor Gipps, 5 March 1839,

116 NSWSA: NRS 905, [4/2492.1] 40/5410, Sarah Bell to Colonial Secretary, 27 May 1840 and attached statement from Kinnear Robertson, Colonial Surgeon. Kesiah Plough: 'Progress of the Colony - First Six Months of 1840', *The South Australian Register,* 18 July 1840, p.5, col. 1-3. http://nla.gov.au/nla.news-article27441650, accessed 10 August 2021.

117 *New South Wales Government Gazette,* 28 August 1839, No. 444, p. 964, col. 1.; 9 October 1839, No 456, p. 1142, col. 2; 27 May 1840, No 30, p.519, col. 2. http://nla. gov.au/nla.news-page12581662 http://nla.gov.au/nla.news-page12581833 http:// nla.gov.au/nla.news-page14286580, accessed 10 August 2021.

118 NSWSA: NRS 905, [4/2401.1] 38/1312, Sarah Bell to Pieter Campbell, 7 December 1838. St John's Parramatta, Marriages 1790-1966, 17 November 1838. ancestry. com.au. NSW. St John's Parramatta, Marriages, 1790-1966. Accessed 15 July 2017. J.C. Byrne, *Twelve Years' Wanderings in the British Colonies, from 1835 to 1847*, London, Bentley, 1848, pp. 230-31.

119 NSWSA: NRS 905, [4/2451.3] 39/6874, Sarah Bell to Governor, 17 June 1839. 'Supreme Court', *Commercial Journal and Advertiser*, 5 May 1838, p.2, col. 4. http:// nla.gov.au/nla.news-article226459311, accessed 10 August 2021.

120 NSWSA: NRS 905, [4/2492.1] 40/217 7, Mary Horn to Mrs Cockrane [Corcoran], 26 February 1840, Charles Forbes to Colonial Secretary, 27 February 1840.

121 NSWSA: NRS 905, [4/2492.1] 40/4876, John Clarke to Thomas Bell, 13 May 1840, Charles Forbes to Colonial Secretary, 15 May 1840.

122 NSWSA, Colonial Secretary, *Returns of the Department of Female Factory Parramatta, 1836-1843.* 4/7327, Reel 702. Five turnkeys from 1838 to 1839 and then only one female turnkey listed. Mary Corcoran appointed sub matron in 1840 with messengers, overseers of laundry, needle room and washing. NSWSA: NRS 905, [4/ 2359.1] 38/9840, [4/2451.3] 39/5322, Sarah Bell to Colonial Secretary, 12 September 1838 with note by Pieter Campbell. Sarah Bell to Colonial Secretary, 6 May 1839. An additional clerk not appointed as Thomas Linehan clerk at Factory, August 1837 to May 1839, and John Johnson, June 1839 to October 1842.

123 NSWSA: Colonial Secretary; NRS 905, 1826-1982, 4/2451.3, [39/1835], Sarah Bell to Colonial Secretary, 7 February 1839.

124 HRA, Ser. 1 Vol. 21, 1 October 1840, p. 6. *New South Wales Government Gazette*, 8 January 1841, p.33, col. 1. http://nla.gov.au/nla.news-article230105635   accessed 30 April 2018.

125 'Aiding a Good Intention', *Sydney Gazette and New South Wales Advertiser*, 1 October 1842, p. 2.col. 4. 'He therefore directed that she should be accommodated ... at Mrs. Bell's academy for young ladies at Parramatta, commonly called the Female Factory.' http://nla.gov.au/nla.news-article2557465 . 'State of the Female Factory, at Parramatta, on 1st July, 1842, *New South Wales Government Gazette*, 5 July 1842, p.975, col. 2. http://nla.gov.au/nla.news-article230361099 accessed 10 August 2021. HRA, Ser. 1 Vol 22, 20 May 1843, pp. 736, 740, 743.

126 HRA, Ser. 1, Vol. 21, 1 October 1840, p. 5. In 1842, the *Insolvency Act* enacted with many in dire financial straits. Hughes and Hosking had best Government contracts in Sydney became insolvent in September 1843, disrupting government contracts and bringing down creditors such as Bank of Australasia.

127 'Female Factory', *The Sydney Gazette and New South Wales Advertiser,* 26 January 1841, p.4, col.3. http://nla.gov.au/nla.news-article2552355 accessed 10 August 2021. NSWSA: NRS 905, [4/2530.2] 41/2265, [4/2610.1], [No number], Sarah Bell to Colonial Secretary, 18 February 1841, Note by Governor Gipps, 20 February 1841. Washing by E Deas Thomson, 19 January 1841. HRA, S.1, Vol 23, 20 May 1843, p.741.

128 NSWSA: NRS 905, [4/2492.1] 40/6886 and enclosed 40/4714, 40/5342, 40/7470, Thomas Bell to Charles Forbes, 13 April 1840, 30 May 1840 and 20 June 1840, Charles Forbes to Deputy Commissioner, General Charles Forbes to Colonial Secretary, 11 July 1840, Miller to Colonial Secretary 31 July 1840.

129 HRA, Ser. 1, Vol 22, 20 May 1843, pp. 741-2, 747. Includes Despatches 76 and 77 to Lord Stanley. Detail of income Appendix 4. HRA, Ser. 1, Vol 22, 20 November 1846, pp. 263-64.

130 NSWSA: NRS 905, [4,2574.1] 42/2322 Enclosing 42/1308 Note by Governor Gipps, 13 February 1842.

131 Golder, H, *Politics and Patronage and Public Works*, p. 84.

132 NSWSA: NRS 905, [4/2530.2] 40/7879, 41/557 Enclosing 40/12,104, Sarah Bell to Colonial Secretary, 10 August 1840, Colonial Secretary to Crown Solicitor, 7 January 1839, Sydney Cotton to Colonial Secretary, 13 January 1841.

133 NSWSA: NRS 905, [4/2574.1] 42/35 and 42/4529, 42/4529, 42/301 and 42/35, Enclosed 42/4471, 42/4529, 42/837, 42/35, Enclosed 42/4471, Sarah Bell to Colonial Secretary, 3 February 1842 and 22 June 1842; James Patchett to Governor Gipps, 17 January 1842 and 1 June 1842; William August Miles to Colonial Secretary, 29 January 1842; William Macpherson's reference, undated.

134 NSWSA: Colonial Secretary; NRS 905, Main series of letters received 1826-1982, 4/2530.2, [41/5874, Enclosed 41/5681], Sydney Cotton to Colonial Secretary, 20 June 1841; Sarah Bell to John Forrester, 9 June 1841, John Forrester to Governor Gipps, 11 June 1841

135 NSWSA: NRS 905, [4/2530.2] 41/7003, 41/7726, Sydney Cotton to Private Secretary, 26 July 1841. Sydney Cotton to Private Secretary, 22 August 1841. 'Runaways

from the Factory', *The Sydney Gazette and New South Wales Advertiser*, 18 December 1841, p.3, col.2. http://nla.gov.au/nla.news-page695482 accessed 10 August 2021.

136 NSWSA: NRS 905, [4/2610.1] 43/7044, 43/4608 Gilbert Eliott to Colonial Secretary, 28 September 1843, Sarah Bell to Colonial Secretary, 19 June 1843, Patrick Hill's and Fergus Hathorn's Colonial Surgeons' Certificates.

137 'State of the Female Factory, at Parramatta, on 1st October, 1842', *New South Wales Government Gazette*, 4 October 1842, p.1470, col. 2. http://nla.gov.au/nla.news-page12500878 accessed 10 August 2021. HRA, Ser. 1, Vol 22, 20 May 1843, pp.736-7. Millbank Prison in Millbank, Westminster, London was a holding facility for convicted prisoners before transported.

138 Sisters of Charity of Australia Congregational Archives, SER/752/1, *The Annals of the Irish Sisters of Charity in Australia 1838-1882*, p. 74.

139 HRA, Ser. 1, Vol 22, 20 May 1843, pp.737-738. Board made up of Deputy Commissary General (William Miller), Principal Superintendent of Convicts (Captain John McLean)) and a medical officer (Patrick Harnett). Report of Board at Appendix 2 of Despatch is missing.

140 HRA, Ser. 1, 12 April 1844, p. 535-36, Enclosure Mr C E Trevelyan to Under Secretary of State James Stephen, 26 March 1844.

141 NSWSA: NRS 905, [4, 2574.1] 42/3752 Enclosed 42/3419 with No Number, Pat Hill to Philip Turner, Commissariat Office, Parramatta, 26 April 1842. Philip Turner to William Miller, 4 May 1842. William Miller to Colonial Secretary, 6 May and 11 May 1842, Philip Turner to William Miller, 13 May 1842, Pat Hill Memorandum, 20 May 1842, Governor Gipps memos, 2 and 6 May 1842. HRA, Ser. 1, Vol. 22, 20 May 1843, pp, 737-38.

142 HRA, Ser.1, Vol 23, 12 April, 1844, pp. 537-38. Includes Sub-enclosure No.1, Dep. Commissary-General Miller to Colonial Secretary, 20 October 1843.

143 NSWSA: NRS 905, [4, 2574.1] No number, [4/2610.1] No number, Advertisement for NSW Government Gazette 12 November 1842 by Governor Gipps, 10 November, 1842; Edward Deas Thomson to Colonial Secretary's Office, *Female Servants*, 28 February 1843. 'State of the Female Factory on the 1st of February, 1843', *New South Wales Government Gazette*, 3 February 1843, p. 195. 811 women and 191 children on 3 February 1843. http://nla.gov.au/nla.news-article230102930 accessed 10 August 2021. HRA, Ser. 1, Vol 22, 20 May 1843, p. 738.

144 NSWSA: NRS 905 [4/2610.1], 43/1448, 43/1336, 43/1347, Eliott to Governor, 18 and 19 February, 1843.

145 HRA, Ser. 1, Vol 22, 20 May 1843, p. 739.

146 'Country News, Parramatta Factory', *The Australian,* 22 February 1843, p.2, col. 7. .http://nla.gov.au/nla.news-article37115987 accessed 10 August 2021.

147 NSWSA: NRS 905, [4/2610.1] 43/1488, 43/1488, Enclosed 43/1347, Royal Engineer Office to Colonial Secretary, 23 February 1843. Memorandum from Governor Gipps, 20 February 1843.

148 NSWSA: NRS 905, [4/2610.1] 43/2610, Gilbert Eliott to Colonial Secretary, 5 April 1843.

149 NSWSA: NRS 905, [4/2610.1] 43/6476, Mary Corcoran's police record, 22 June 1838.

150 NSWSA: NRS 905, [4/2359] 37/8144, [4/2451.3] 39/67, Sarah Bell to Colonial Secretary, 23 August 1837, Sarah Bell to Colonial Secretary, 2 January 1839. Sarah requested Mary Corcoran be paid £50.

151 NSWSA: NRS 905, [4/2574. 1] 42/3752 Enclosed 42/3868. Sarah Bell to Colonial Secretary, 20 May 1842. Anne Edgely or Edgeley.

152 NSWSA: NRS 905, [4/2610.1] 43/6476 Enclosed 43/6003, Sarah Bell to Gilbert Eliott, 9 August 1843.

153 NSWSA: NRS 905, [4/2610.1] 43/6476, Note from Governor Gipps to Colonial Secretary, 17 August 1843. HRA, S1, Vol 23, 12 April, 1844, pp. 537-38. Charges of Embezzlement by Mrs Corcoran, Sub-enclosure No.2, 21 October 1843. Mr Allan, possibly Rev. James Allan, minister of Presbyterian Church arrived in NSW on 5 October 1837 and took over congregation at Parramatta.Mr Allan later joined the Anglican Church.

154 NSWSA: NRS 905, [4/2610.1] 43/6476, Report of Board on charges against Sub Matron of Female Factory, 5 September 1843, Minutes of the Evidence for Report of Board of Enquiry.

155 'Convict Records, Isabella' https://convictrecords.com.au/ships There is an Elizabeth Taylor on the *Isabella (1840)*. Accessed 10 August 2021.

156 Lord Stanley to Governor Gipps, HRA, S1, Vol 23, 12 April, 1844, pp. 537-38. Charges of Embezzlement by Mrs Corcoran, Sub-enclosure No.2, 21 October 1843.

157 NSWSA: NRS 905, [4/2610.1] 43/6476, Report of Board on charges against Sub Matron of Female Factory, 5 September 1843, Minutes of the Evidence for Report of Board of Enquiry.

158 HRA, Ser. 1, Vol 23, 1 October 1843, p. 171. NSWSA: NRS 905, [4/2610.1] 43/6476, No Number, Colonial Secretary Report of Board of Enquiry, Memo from Governor Gipps, 29 September 1843.

159 'State of the Female Factory, Parramatta, on the 1st of September, 1843', *New South Wales Government Gazette*, 5 September 1843, p. 1149. col. 1. http://nla.gov.au/nla.news-article230126703 accessed 10 August 2021.

160 HRA, Ser. 1, 12 April 1844, p. 533-36, Enclosure Mr C E Trevelyan to Under Secretary of State, James Stephen, 26 March 1844.

161 Dr Anderson was resident surgeon at Parramatta from 1829-1841 and a magistrate. John Blaxland was brother of Gregory Blaxland who, with Wentworth and Lawson, were first white people to cross Blue Mountains. Captain Robert Gerald Moffat waa a magistrate at Parramatta from 1834 to 1843 and then took up land on the Darling Downs.

162 *Callaghan's Diary: the 1840s Sydney diary of Thomas Callaghan.* 2005, p. 185. 'Notice in the Supreme Court of New South Wales', *New South Wales Government Gazette*, 20 March 1833, p, 101, col. 2. http://nla.gov.au/nla.news-article230389901 George Nichols was on the Parramatta District Council and in 1848 was elected to the Legislative Council.

163 Details of hearing are taken from two articles in *The Australian*. Questions asked by the prosecution and defence during the examination and cross-examination, as well as those asked by the bench, are not always clear which could lead to a misinterpretation of some of responses. 'Country News Parramatta', *The Australian*, 10 October, p. 4, col. 1. and 17 October, 1843, p. 3, cols 4-7 and p. 4, cols, 1-4. http://nla.gov.au/nla.news-article37113393 http://nla.gov.au/nla.news-page4255586 http://nla.gov.au/nla.news-article37118305 accessed 10 August 2021.

164 A. Cowie, A J, 'A History of Women's Real Property Rights', 2009, *Australian Journal of Gender and Law, Article 6,* http://www5.austlii.edu.au/au/journals/AUJlGendLaw/2009/6.html accessed 10 August 2021.

165 'State of the Female Factory, Parramatta, on Tuesday, 14th September, 1841 and 21st September, 1841' *New South Wales Government Gazette,* 17 September 1841, p. 1259, col. 2., 24 September 1841, p. 1299, col. 1. http://nla.gov.au/nla.news-article230395255 http://nla.gov.au/nla.news-article230395367 accessed 10 August 2021.

166 https://convictrecords.com.au/convicts/edge/jane/46366

167 Lucy Martin does not appear in convict records or the Female Factory Convict List by Beth Matthews and Anne Mathews. https://parramattafemalefactories.files.wordpress.com/2017/01/female-factory-womens-list-bmam1901.pdf accessed 10 August 2021.

168 'In the Insolvent Estate of Robert Miller, and John Hamilton, of Parramatta' *New South Wales Government Gazette,* 23 February 1844, p. 339, col. 2. http://nla.gov.au/nla.news-article230146505 . Robert Miller and Co became insolvent in February 1844. John Hughes and John Hosking opened steam flour mill in 1833 in Darling Harbour on Sussex Street which was underinsured and when destroyed by fire in March 1841, Hughes and Hosking borrowed extensively from Bank of Australia to recoup losses but failed and bankrupt in 1843, victim of the economic depression of the early 1840s and led to collapse of Bank of Australia, to which they owed more than £155,000. Hughes continued trading after 1846 with a new Albion Steam Mill on his estate in Surry Hills. https://dictionaryofsydney.org/structure/albion_mills_darling_harbour accessed 10 August 2021.

169 NSWSA: NRS 905, [4/2610.1] 43/6476, Mary Corcoran's police record, 22 June 1838. M O'Sullivan and M. Doyle, 'A Convict Remembered: Mary Corcoran', In *Journal of the Australian Catholic Historical Society,* Vol, 20, 1 January 1999, pp. 31-40. https://search.informit.org/doi/10.3316/IELAPA.200004088 . 'Pioneer Sites' https://pioneersites.wordpress.com/journey-with-us-to-the-pioneer-sites/ accessed 10 August 2021.

170 'Family Notices', *The Weekly Register of Politics, Facts and General Literature,* 4 November 1843, p. 230. http://nla.gov.au/nla.news-page22336029 accessed 10 August 2021.

171 'The New Court House', *Australasian Chronicle,* 8 February 1842, p.2, col. 6. http://nla.gov.au/nla.news-article31734967 accessed 10 August 2021.

172 'The Great Trial', *The Sydney Morning Herald,* 11 April 1845, p. 2, col. 2. http://nla.gov.au/nla.news-article12878679 accessed 6 January 2021.

173 NSWSA: Supreme Court of NSW; NRS 880, Papers and Depositions, Supreme Court Sydney and on Circuit, 1824-1946. [9/6336] Supreme Court Information,

Jury list reduced. 'Law Intelligence, Supreme Court', *The Sydney Morning Herald*, 29 January 1844, p.2, col. 2. http://nla.gov.au/nla.news-article28651045   accessed 10 August 2021. NSWSA: NRS 905, [4/2649.2] 44/7187, John Plunkett to the Colonial Secretary, 13 February 1844. Similar arrangements were entered for Dennis Hannan and John Hamilton.

174 'Functions of the Attorney General', *The Examiner* 6 September 1845, p. 34, col. 2. http://nla.gov.au/nla.news-article228062753 'Law Intelligence Central Criminal Court', *The Sydney Morning Herald*, 19 July 1844, p. 4, col. 1. http://nla.gov.au/nla.news-article12409455 . 'Parramatta Factory Cases', *The Australian*, 8 July 1844, p. 3. col. 3. http://nla.gov.au/nla.news-article37122521 accessed 10 August 2021.

175 Arthur Hodgson wrote in *The Queenslander,* 1 April 1899, p. 609, col., 3. http://nla.gov.au/nla.news-article20858171 that Thomas Bell was still living at Parramatta in 1845. NSWSA, Colonial Secretary, NRS 905, Main series of letters received 1826-1982, 45/1010, Sarah Bell to Henry Parker, 7 February 1845.

176 'Law Intelligence Central Criminal Court', *The Sydney Morning Herald*, 18 July 1845, p. 2. col. 4-5. http://nla.gov.au/nla.news-article12880949 accessed 10 August 2021.

177 'Functions of the Attorney General', *The Examiner*, 6 September 1845, p. 3, col. 2, 3. http://nla.gov.au/nla.news-article228062753 accessed 10 August 2021.

178 'Law Intelligence. Central Criminal Court.' *The Australian*, 7 October 1845, p. 3, col. 3. http://nla.gov.au/nla.news-article37155936 accessed 10 August 2021.

179 'Windsor', *The Sydney Morning Herald*, 7 October 1844, p.5, col. 1. http://nla.gov.au/nla.news-article28651272 accessed 10 August 2021.

180 NSWSA: Colonial Secretary; NRS 906, Special bundles. [4/6670.4] Brief in Regina v Bell and Hamilton (fraud at the Female Factory) and Hannan and Hamilton (fraud at Parramatta Convict Hospital), 1842-45.   HRA, Ser. 1, Vol. 24, 28 February 1846, Enclosure Attorney General Plunkett to Colonial Secretary Thomson, 20 January 1846, p. 792.

181 NSWSA: Supreme Court of NSW, NRS 880, Papers and Depositions, Supreme Court Sydney and on Circuit, 1824-1946. [9/6336]; Supreme Court Information, Regina v Bell and Hamilton (fraud at the Female Factory) and Hannan and Hamilton (fraud at Parramatta Convict Hospital), 1842-4, Deposition of Andrew Kell, 13 October 1845, Statement of Robert Miller, nd., E. Courtney, 20 May 1845.

182 'Law Intelligence Central Criminal Court.' *The Australian*, 9 October 1845, p. 3, col. 5. http://nla.gov.au/nla.news-article37159363 accessed 10 August 2021.

183 'Supreme Court Scene', *The Australian* 11 October 1845 page 3, col. 6. http://nla.gov.au/nla.news-article37156786 accessed 10 August 2021.

184 'The Unfathomable Factory Case', *The Cumberland Times and Western Advertiser*, 18 October 1845, p.2, col. 3.http://nla.gov.au/nla.news-article228065934 accessed 10 August 2021.

185 'Law Proceedings', *The Sydney Morning Herald*, 11 October 1845, p. 2, col 3. http://nla.gov.au/nla.news-article12882772 accessed 10 August 2021.   *'L-A-W, Law', The Sydney Morning Herald*, 15 October 1845, p. 3, col 2. http://nla.gov.au/nla.news-article12882835 accessed 10 August 2021.

186 NSWSA: Supreme Court of NSW, NRS 880, Papers and Depositions, Supreme Court Sydney and on Circuit, 1824-1946. [9/6336]; Supreme Court Information, Regina v Bell and Hamilton (fraud at the Female Factory) and Hannan and Hamilton (fraud at Parramatta Convict Hospital), 1842-4, John Johnstone to Attorney General, 6 November 1845.   NSWSA: Colonial Secretary; NRS 905, [4/2708.2] Supreme Court. 45/7642 Attorney General to Colonial Secretary, 21 October 1845.

187 NSWSA: Colonial Secretary; NRS 905, [4/2708.2] Supreme Court. 45/4248, 45/7642, 45/8892. G. P. F. Gregory (Prothonotary and Registrar of the Supreme Court of NSW) to Governor Gipps, 9 June 1845. Mr Cox to Judges, 15 October 1845. Justices Stephens and Dickinson to Colonial Secretary, 10 December 1845; Colonial Secretary to Justices, 11 December 1845.

188 Supreme Court of NSW; NRS 880, Papers and Depositions, Supreme Court Sydney on Circuit, 1824-1946. [9/6336] Gordon Gwynne to Supreme Court, NSW, 9 December 1845. 'The Parramatta Factory Case', *The Maitland Mercury and Hunter River General Advertiser*, 20 December 1845, p.4, col. 1. http://nla.gov.au/nla. news-article677255 'Legislative Council', *The Sydney Morning Herald*, 17 October 1846, p2. cols, 4, 5, and 6. http://nla.gov.au/nla.news-article12892934 accessed 10 August 2021.

189 HRA, Ser. 1, Vol 24, p.792-94 Including Enclosure Attorney-General to Colonial Secretary Thomson, 20 January, 1846.

190 'The Parramatta Factory Case', *Bell's Life in Sydney and Sporting Reviewer*, 14 February 1846, p.2, col. 3. http://nla.gov.au/nla.news-article59765735 accessed 10 August 2021.

191 HRA, Ser. 1, Vol 25, 5 June 1846, p. 84.

192 'Died', *The Sydney Morning Herald*, 29 December 1845, p.3, col. 1 http://nla.gov.au/ nla.news-article12884383   'To be Let or Sold', *The Sydney Morning Herald*, 6 January 1846, p.4, col. 1.   http://nla.gov.au/nla.news-article12884508 *The Queenslander*, 7 January 1898, p.48, col. 2. http://nla.gov.au/nla.news-article20854982 accessed 10 August 2021.   Joshua may have been working in a Mr Seaton's solicitor's office in Sydney. John and Marmaduke not in The Kings School Register for this period.

193 Note on telegram from John Alexander Bell to his wife Frances Bell, 23 October 1893. UQFL79, Box 4, Folder 8, Fryer Library, The University of Queensland Library.

194 The Darling Downs District stretched from the Great Dividing Range in the east to the Clarence River in the south with its northern and western boundaries not clearly defined. Commissioner had control over more than 26,000 square miles (7 million hectares) and his duties included issuing pasturing and business licences, maintaining law and order (with only a small unit of Border Police) and sending statistical reports to the Colonial Secretary.

195 'Jimbour History', *The Queenslander*, 7 January 1898, p.48, col. 2. http://nla.gov.au/ nla.news-article20854982 Charles Dun, William Dun's son, and five men drove 11,000 sheep and 700 cattle from the Namoi River (south of Tamworth) arriving at Jimbour in October 1842.   'Jimbour History', *The Queenslander*, 1 April 1899, p. 609. col. 3. http://nla.gov.au/nla.news-article20858171. Purchase by Thomas Bell is unclear but probably in 1844 or 1845. accessed 10 August 2021. NSWSA.

Depasturing Licences Index 1837-1852, NRS 14363, Item No: [4/102] [4/106], Copy 5078 and 5081, Locality: Darling Downs, Thomas Bell Licence 677 and 833.

196 R Kerkhove, Tribal Alliances with broader agendas? Aboriginal Resistance in southern Queensland's Black War, In *Cosmopolitan Civil Societies Journal*, Vol.6, No.3, 2014. https://epress.lib.uts.edu.au/journals/index.php/mcs/article/view/4218/4491 accessed 10 August 2021.

197 Jimba and Gimba may have been local Aboriginal words for 'good pastures'. Leichhardt, Ludwig, *Journal of an overland expedition in Australia from Moreton Bay to Port Essington, a distance of upwards of 3000 miles, during the years 1844–1845*, University of Sydney Library, 2002. First published 1846.

198 HRA, Ser. 1, vol 22, 20 May 1843, pp. 742, 747. HRA, Ser. 1, vol 25, 30 June 1846, p, 125.

199 HRA, Ser. 1, vol. 25, 20 November 1846, p.263

200 'Dr Leichhardt', *The Maitland Mercury and Hunter River General Advertiser*, 2 January 1847, p.2, col. 5. http://nla.gov.au/nla.news-article686841 accessed 10 August 2021. Jimba was now named Jimbour.

201 Mann, John, *Eight Months with Dr. Leichhardt in the Years 1846–47*, Sydney, Turner and Henderson, 1886, p. 16.

202 HRA, Ser. 1, vol. 25, Sir Charles Fitz Roy to Earl Grey, Despatch 82, 8 April 1847, p.479-80. AJCP, Colonial Office (CO201) Enclousure to Govenor's Dispatch, No28, 8 April, 1847. File 381, AJCP Reel 382-383, pp 95-132. Deputy Commissary General, Thomas Ramsay to Colonial Secretary, 8 and 19 February 1847, Thomas Bell to Thomas Ramsay, 22 January and 18 February, 1847, Declaration of Mr and Mrs Smyth, 27 January 1847, Gilbert Eliott, Visiting Justice to Colonial Secretary, 13 February and 22 March 1847, Pat Hill, Colonial Surgeon to Gilbert Eliott, 13 February 1847, Colonial Secretary to Thomas Ramsay, 23 February 1847.

203 Total Destruction of the Sovereign steam-packet, and Melancholy Loss of Life', *The Sydney Morning Herald*, 27 March 1847, p.1, cols 1-4. http://nla.gov.au/nla.news-article12893901, 'Shipping Intelligence. Arrival.' *The Moreton Bay Courier*, 27 March 1847, p.2, col.1. http://nla.gov.au/nla.news-article3711605. 'Shipping Intelligence. Arrival', *The Moreton Bay Courier*, 24 April 1847, p.2, col.1. http://nla.gov.au/nla.news-article3716275. accessed 10 August 2021.

204 St. Augustine's College', *The Sydney Morning Herald*, 9 November 1850, p. 2, col. 5. http://nla.gov.au/nla.news-article12922420 Accessed 10 August 2021. Among successful students for honours at St. Augustine's College, Canterbury.

205 NSWSA: NRS 905, 49/6988, Thomas Bell to Colonial Secretary, 23 July 1849

206 'Died', *The Sydney Morning Herald*, 13 June 1853, p. 2, col. 6. http://nla.gov.au/nla.news-article12946646 Access 13 January 2021. Sarah Bell's portrait may be a miniature in oil, watercolour or mezzotint,"which professional photographer J. Botterill produced in 1860s in addition to photographs. Botterill was based at the Melbourne address in the late 1870s, putting an even later date on this image. Someone may have given Mr. Botterill a drawing of Sarah, which became the basis of this (possibly watercolour) image.

207 Shipping Intelligence. Arrivals', *The Moreton Bay Courier,* 23 October 1847, p.2, col. 1. http://nla.gov.au/nla.news-article3711581. accessed 10 August 2021. Captain Moffatt and J. Bell travelled on the Tamar to Moreton Bay. Bell Family Bible held by Anita O'Connor in County Galway. Robert Gerald Moffatt, was a captain in the 17th Regiment of Foot posted to NSW from 1830 to 1836. He was a magistrate and commander of the military police in Port Stephens and sold his commission on 19 December 1834. His wife Sarah died in December 1839 and was buried in St John's Cemetery.

208 'Daguerreotype Camera', *The Sydney Morning Herald,* 27 August 1853, p.7, col. 1. http://nla.gov.au/nla.news-article12948457. 'Liberty Plains', *The Sydney Morning Herald,* 26 September, 1853, p.6, col.1. http://nla.gov.au/nla.news-article12949089 accessed 10 August 2021.

209 'Crown Land Sales', *The North Australian, Ipswich and General Advertiser,* 4 December p. 3, 1860. col. 1 1,http,http://nla.gov.au/nla.news-article77433879. accessed 10 August 2021.

210 'Departure', *Queensland Times, Ipswich Herald and General Advertiser,* 26 November 1872, p. 2, col. 3. http://nla.gov.au/nla.news-article123620018   accessed 10 August 2021.

211 'Local and General News', *Queensland Times, Ipswich Herald and General Advertiser,* 7 September 1872, p. 3, col. 1. http://nla.gov.au/nla.news-article123621176 accessed 10 August 2021.

212 'Social and General', *Queensland Times, Ipswich Herald and General Advertiser,* 3 October 1872, p. 3, col. 2. http://nla.gov.au/nla.news-article123621061 accessed 10 August 2021.

Bibliography

Archival Sources

NSWSA: Colonial Secretary, NRS 905, Main series of letters received 1826-1982. Female Factory 1833-1844, [4/2191.3, 4/2234.5, 4/2277.4, 4/2317.2, 4/2359.1, 4/2401.1, 4/2451.3, 4/2492.1, 4/2530.2, 4/2574.1, 4/2610.1, 4/2649.2.].

NSWSA: Colonial Secretary, NRS 905, Main Series of letters received, 1826-1982. [4/2708.2] Supreme Court 45/7642.

NSWSA: Colonial Secretary, NRS 906, Returns of the Department of Female Factory Parramatta, 1836-1843, [4/7327], Reel 702.

NSWSA: Colonial Secretary, NRS 906, Special bundles. [4/6670] Brief in Regina v Bell and Hamilton (fraud at the Female Factory) and Hannan and Hamilton (fraud at the Parramatta Convict Hospital (1842-45).

NSWSA: Colonial Secretary, NRS 909, Letters Received - Governor's Minutes and Memoranda,1834-1850, 4/999, Memoranda 3694, 1836.

NSWSA: Supreme Court of NSW; NRS 880, Papers and Depositions, Supreme Court Sydney and on Circuit, 1824-1946, [96336] Supreme Court Information, Jury list reduced.

National Archives (UK), Governor's Correspondence, 1832 to 1844, File 114, AJCP Reel 1046, (From Records of the Colonial Office, Index of Incoming Correspondence, (CO 714).   https://nla.gov.au/nla.obj-1208748209/view.

State Library of NSW

Bourke family - Papers [M1863], 1809-1855. Diary of Anne Bourke, daughter of Sir Richard Bourke kept on the voyage from England to N.S.W. Canberra : Australian Joint Copying Project, [10—]. M1863.

CO, Series 201, NSW, Original Correspondence, 1783-1900. Enclosure to Governor's Despatches, No 82, 8 April 1847. File 381, AJCP Reel N0: 382-383, pp. 95-132. https://nla.gov.au/nla.obj-1013857978/view

CO, Series 201, NSW, Original Correspondence, 1783-1900. Miscellaneous Individuals, A-F, 1838, File 281, AJCP Reel No: 315-316, 'Parramatta Female Factory 1838: Correspondence between Secretary of State for Colonial Department and the Governors of the Australian Provinces on the Subject of Secondary Punishment'.

Miles, William Alexander, 'Sketches of Europe and Australia', ca. 1834-50'. PXA537.

Various documents collected by Sir William Dixson, including material relating to John Oxley, the Female Factory, the Blaxland family and the New South Wales Executive Council. Item 3 Rules for the Government of the Female Factory drawn up by Sir Richard Bourke, Visiting Magistrate'. 28 February 1839. State Library of NSW.

Watson, Frederick, ed., Australia. Parliament. Library Committee. (1914). *Historical Records of Australia.* http://nla.gov.au/nla.obj-442186184

Books and articles

Ashton, Paul and Wilson, Jacqueline (eds.) *Silent System: Forgotten Australians and the Institutionalisation of Women and Children*, Melbourne, Australian Scholarly, 2014.

Backhouse, James, *A Narrative of a Visit to the Australian Colonies*, London, Hamilton, Adams, and Co, 1843. https://espace.library.uq.edu.au/view/UQ:319336

Barker, Geoff, *The Second Female Factory: 1818-1848*, Parramatta Heritage Centre, 2018. https://historyandheritage.cityofparramatta.nsw.gov.au/blog/2015/07/28/the-second-parramatta-female-factory-1818-1848

Bell, Sir Joshua Peter (1827-1881), Australian Dictionary of Biography. http://adb.anu.edu.au/biography/bell-sir-joshua-peter-2969

Bell v. Pearce [1854] Supreme Court of New South Wales, Moreton Bay, 18 May 1854. https://www.austlii.edu.au/cgi-bin/viewdoc/au/cases/nsw/NSWSupCMB/1854/1.html?context=1

Bryson, J, 'Debtors' prison and the rules of the prison'. *Bar News: The Journal of the NSW Bar Association*, Summer 2019, Dec 2019. https://search.informit.org/doi/epdf/10.3316/informit.914269705077024

Burton, W, *The State of Religion and Education in New South Wales*, London, J Cross, 1840, Appendix, no. 16. https://ia800200.us.archive.org/17/items/stateofreligione00burt/stateofreligione00burt.pdf

Byrne, J C, *Twelve Years' Wanderings in the British Colonies, from 1835 to 1847*, London, Bentley, 1848.

Callaghan, Thomas, *Callaghan's Diary: The 1840s Sydney diary of Thomas Callaghan.* Sydney, Francis Forbes Society for Australian Legal History, 2005.

Callaghan, Thomas, *The Acts and Ordinances of The Governor & Council of New South Wales and Acts of Parliament Enacted for, and applied to, the Colony, 2 vols, Sydney, WJ Row*, 1844.

Cowie, Andrew James, 'A History of Women's Real Property Rights', *Australian Journal of Gender and Law, Article 6, 2009*, http://www5.austlii.edu.au/au/journals/AUJlGendLaw/2009/6.html

Evans, Raymond, 'Creating 'an Object of Real Terror': the tabling of the Bigge Report', *In Turning Points in Australian History*, Sydney, University of New South Wales Press, 2009.

Frost, Lucy and Maxwell-Stewart, Hamish (eds.), *Chain letters: narrating convict lives*, Melbourne, Melbourne University Press, 2001.

Golder, Hilary, *Politics, Patronage and Public Works: the Administration of New South Wales, Volume 1, 1842-1900*, Sydney, University of New South Wales Press, 2005.

Harrison, Jennifer, *Shackled: Female Convicts at Moreton Bay 1826-1839*, Melbourne, Anchor Books, 2016.

Heath, L., (MA Thesis), 'The Female Factories of New South Wales and Van Diemen's Land: an Examination of their role in Control, Punishment and Reformation of Prisoners between 1804 and 1854'. Canberra, ANU, n.d. https://openresearch-repository.anu.edu.au/bitstream/1885/10869/4/Heath_L_1978.pdf

Hendrikson, Gail, *Conviction: The 1827 Fight for Rights at the Parramatta Female Factory*, Rowan Tree Published Books, The Parramatta Heritage Centre, n.d.

Kerkhove, Ray, 'Tribal Alliances with broader agendas? Aboriginal Resistance in southern Queensland', In *Cosmopolitan Civil Societies Journal*, Vol.6, No.3, 2014. https://epress.lib.uts.edu.au/journals/index.php/mcs/article/view/4218/4491

Leichhardt, Ludwig, *Journal of an overland expedition in Australia from Moreton Bay to Port Essington, a distance of upwards of 3000 miles, during the years 1844–1845*, University of Sydney Library, 2002. First published 1846.

Lloyd's Register of British and Foreign Shipping, London, Society for the Registry of Shipping, 1931. https://www.google.com/books/edition/_/MzkSAAAAYAAJ

McConville, S., *Irish Political Prisoners, 1848-1922*, London, Routledge, 2003,

Mann, John, *Eight Months with Dr. Leichhardt in the Years 1846-47*, Sydney, Turner and Henderson, 1886

Maynard, Margaret, *Fashioned from Penury: Dress as Cultural Practice in Colonial Australia*, CUP, 1994.

Nicholson, Ian Hawkins, *Shipping Arrivals and Departures Tasmania Vol 1 1803-1833*, Canberra Roebuck Society, 1985.

O'Sullivan, Moira and Doyle, M Claudia, 'A Convict Remembered: Mary Corcoran', *Journal of the Australian Catholic Historical Society*, Vol 20 1999, pp 31-40. 9. https://search.informit.org/doi/10.3316/IELAPA.200004088

Oxley, Deborah, *Convict Maids: the Forced Migration of Women to Australia.* Melbourne, Cambridge University Press, 1996.

Philips, D., *William Augustus Miles (1796-1851): crime, policing and moral entrepreneurship in England and Australia*, Melbourne, History Department, University of Melbourne (University of Melbourne history monographs: no. 30), 2001, pp. 182-88.

Phillips, Joyce, *Old Ipswich Days: Joshua Peter Bell and the Ipswich Connection*, Ipswich, Joyce Phillips, 2008.

Rushen, Elizabeth, *Colonial Duchesses: the migration of Irish women to New South Wales before the Great Famine*, by Sydney, Anchor Books, 2014.

Rushen, Elizabeth and McIntyre, Perry, *Fair Game: Australia's first immigrant women*, Sydney, Anchor Books, 2010.

Rushen, Elizabeth and McIntyre, Perry, *The Merchant's Women, Sydney, Anchor Books, 2008.*

Rushen, Elizabeth, *Single and Free: Female Migration to Australia, 1833-1837*, Melbourne, Australian Scholarly Publishing, 2003.

Salt, Annette, *Those Outcast Women: The Female Factory 1821-1848*, Hale & Iremonger, Sydney, 1984.

Sir George Gipps, Australian Dictionary of Biography.
http://adb.anu.edu.au/biography/gipps-sir-george-2098

Sisters of Charity of Australia Congregational Archives, SER/752/1, *The Annals of the Irish Sisters of Charity in Australia 1838-1882*, Irish Sisters of Charity, Potts Point, Sydney.

Smith, T, 'Cumberland Hospital - the early years', *Parramatta Female Factory Friends Newsletter,* Issue no 11, October - November 2016.

Tedeschi, Mark, *Murder at Myall Creek,: the trial that defined a nation*, Sydney, Simon & Schuster, 2017.

Waddy L., *The King's School, 1831-1981: An account*, Parramatta, The Council of The King's School, 1981,

Waugh, Max, *Forgotten Hero: Richard Burke, Irish Governor of New South Wales 1831-1837*, Melbourne, Scholarly Publishing, 2005.

Women Transported: Life in Australia's Convict Female Factories, Parramatta, 2008. https://historyandheritage.cityofparramatta.nsw.gov.au/sites/phh/files/field/media/file/2020-09/women-transported.pdf

Yeend, P., *King's School Register, 1831-1990*, Parramatta, Kings School, 1990.

Index

Academy *for* Young Ladies

www.ingramcontent.com/pod-product-compliance
Lightning Source LLC
Chambersburg PA
CBHW032031050726
47590CB00006B/2376